Home and Away

Home and Away

Contextual Theology and Local Practice

Edited by
STEPHEN BURNS *and* CLIVE PEARSON

☙PICKWICK *Publications* • Eugene, Oregon

HOME AND AWAY
Contextual Theology and Local Practice

Copyright © 2013 Wipf and Stock Publishers. All rights reserved. Except for brief quotations in critical publications or reviews, no part of this book may be reproduced in any manner without prior written permission from the publisher. Write: Permissions, Wipf and Stock Publishers, 199 W. 8th Ave., Suite 3, Eugene, OR 97401.

Pickwick Publications
An Imprint of Wipf and Stock Publishers
199 W. 8th Ave., Suite 3
Eugene, OR 97401

www.wipfandstock.com

ISBN 13: 978-1-61097-887-3

Cataloguing-in-Publication data:

Home and away : contextual theology and local practice / edited by Stephen Burns and Clive Pearson.

x + 154 pp. ; 23 cm. Includes bibliographical references.

ISBN 13: 978-1-61097-887-3

1. Christianity—Australia. 2. Christianity and culture—Australia. I. Burns, Stephen (1970–). II. Pearson, Clive. III. Title.

BR1480 H60 2013

Manufactured in the USA

Contents

Preface · vii

List of Contributors · ix

1. Home and Away: Faith an Identity in Diaspora
   —*Clive Pearson* · 1

2. Postal-Code 2016/2017: Redfern/Waterloo in South Sydney
   —*Dorothy McCrae-McMahon* · 15

3. Postal-Code 3000: Imaging Sacred Space—*Simon Holt* · 24

4. Cross of Flowers: Echoes of Times Past or a Signpost toward a Future?—*Matthew Wilson* · 35

5. For Christ's Sake! Post-Coding Christ-Talk
   —*Michael N. Jagessar* · 48

6. From Seclusion to Inclusion: Envisioning God's Kingdom for the Mentally Ill—*Mary Pearson* · 72

7. Wandering—*Stephen Burns* · 84

8. Displacing Theology: God-Talk in an "Age of Migration"
   —*Susanna Snyder* · 104

9. Homemaking in the Diaspora: From Displaced Guest to Responsible Host—*Seforosa Carroll* · 124

10. Crossing Postal Codes in Early Modern Japan:
    The Stories of Tamura Naomi and Osaka Motokichiro
    —*Thomas Hastings* · 137

Preface

HOME AND AWAY IS a cluster of exercises in contextual theology, in different but related modes. An initial stream of essays looks at the significance of postal-codes as a way of mapping local areas as situations for pastoral ministry and theological reflection. A second, but not ancillary, stream of essays considers the local within a range of glocal and global dynamics, with particular attention to human migration, diaspora and communication media. The essays do not unfold a single trajectory of thought about context, and at various points they indirectly question and challenge each other. That they are collected together and juxtaposed can therefore deepen others' reflection on "postal-codes."

The pieces meld into an international and ecumenical conversation about contemporary Christian understanding and ministry. The conversation includes voices from North America, Europe and Austral/Asia, where the essays find their weight of gravity, in as much as most focus on Austral/Asia (and especially Australia), and some are written from outside Asia about Asia. Although open ended, and constantly criss-crossing questions from one context to another, the collection is emphatic in its common conviction that attention to very local circumstance is crucial, just as are wider views of a locality's position in broader "flows."

Contributors

STEPHEN BURNS is Research Fellow in Public and Contextual Theology at Charles Sturt University. He is a priest in the orders of the Church of England, and his publications include *Liturgy* (SCM Studyguide, 2006), *Worship in Context: Liturgical Theology, Children and the City* (2006), *Exchanges of Grace: Essays in Honour of Ann Loades* (coeditor, with Natalie K. Watson, 2008), *The Edge of God: New Liturgical Texts and Contexts in Conversation* (coeditor, with Nicola Slee and Michael N. Jagessar, 2008), *Christian Worship in Australia: Inculturating the Liturgical Tradition* (coeditor, with Anita Monro, 2009), *Presiding Like a Woman* (coeditor, with Nicola Slee, 2010), and *Christian Worship: Postcolonial Perspectives* (coauthor, with Michael N. Jagessar, 2011). He is book reviews editor of the *Australian Journal of Liturgy*.

SEFOROSA CARROLL is a minister of the Word in the Uniting Church in Australia, and Convenor of its Working Group on Relationships with Other Faiths. She is a doctoral candidate at Charles Sturt University.

THOMAS JOHN HASTINGS is Associate Director of the Centre for Theological Inquiry at Princeton, New Jersey. He is an ordained minister of Word and sacrament in the Presbyterian Church (USA), and his publications include *Practical Theology and the One Body of Christ: Toward a Missional-Ecumenical Model* (2007).

SIMON HOLT is Senior Minister of Collins Street Baptist Church in Melbourne. His publications include *The Bible and the Business of Life: Essays in Honour of Robert J. Banks* (coeditor, with Gordon Preece, 2004) and *God Next Door: Spirituality and Mission in the Neighbourhood* (2007).

MICHAEL N. JAGESSAR is national Moderator of the Assembly of the United Reformed Church, and a minister of the United Reformed Church.

His publications include: *Black Theology in Britain: A Reader* (coeditor, with Anthony G. Reddie, 2007), *Black British Postcolonial Theology* (coeditor, with Anthony G. Reddie, 2007), *The Edge of God: New Liturgical Texts and Contexts in Conversation* (coeditor, with Nicola Slee and Stephen Burns, 2008), and *Christian Worship: Postcolonial Perspectives* (coauthor, with Stephen Burns, 2011). He is book reviews editor of *Black Theology: An International Journal*.

DOROTHY MCRAE-MCMAHON, AM, is a minister of the Word in the Uniting Church in Australia, in which she serves in the Sydney presbytery. Her publications include *Liturgies for the Journey of Life* (2000), *In This Hour: Liturgies for Pausing* (2001), *Liturgies for Life's Particular Moments* (2001), *Liturgies for Daily Life* (2004), *Liturgies for High Days* (2006), and *Liturgies for the Young in Years* (2007).

CLIVE PEARSON is Associate Professor and Head of School in Theology at Charles Sturt University. He is a minister of the Word in the Uniting Church in Australia. His publications include *Faith in a Hyphen: Cross-cultural Theologies Down Under* (editor, 2004), *Thirty Years of Korean Ministry in Australia* (coeditor, with Myong Duk Yang, 2004), and *Scholarship and Fierce Sincerity: Henry D. A. Major and the Face of Modern Anglicanism* (coauthor, with Allan Davidson and Peter Lineman, 2007). He is editor of *Cross-culture: A Journal of Theology and Ministerial Practice*.

MARY PEARSON is a minister of the Word in the Uniting Church in Australia, and is Mental Health Chaplain at the Concord Centre for Mental Health, Sydney.

SUSANNA SNYDER is Assistant Professor at Episcopal Divinity School, Cambridge, Massachusetts, and a priest in the orders of the Church of England. Her publications include *Asylum-Seeking, Migration and Church* (2012).

MATTHEW WILSON is a minister of the Word in the Uniting Church in Australia, in which he serves in the Ku-ring-gai presbytery.

1

Home and Away
Faith an Identity in Diaspora

Clive Pearson

ON USING POSTAL-CODES IN THEOLOGY

SOME YEARS AGO ANDREW Dutney called for a theology that bore the postalmark Australia.[1] The intention was to construct a contextual theology that respected the lines of continuity and discontinuity between the settler societies of the south and the apparently more universal, classical shape of beliefs developed in the north over a longer period of time. On this occasion Dutney did not make use of the analogy of the antipodes but did presuppose that the ways of doing theology and the forms received had not always addressed the soteriological necessity of life down under.

This metaphor of the postalmark had suggested itself to Dutney on the basis of his reading of the Pauline outward correspondence in the New Testament. Here the conventions of letter writing and reading an atlas were skillfully brought together in order to explore the "universalities of being 'in Christ' and the particularities of being 'in Australia.'" Dutney had made his call for such a theology while thinking about national identity and its

---
1. Dutney, "Postmark Australia," 3–4.

intersection with faith on the occasion of the bicentenary of Australia in 1988. The timing was half a decade pre-Google. There was electronic mail but its use was relatively limited and the postalmark was still primarily an aid to communication. Now its function is more constrained but its close cousin, the postal-code, has acquired a new lease of life.

The postal-code can serve as a tool for market research and sociological study. It locates and situates us. The postal-code places us on the map and reveals telling tales of our neighbourhoods. It allows for the study of consumer habits, lifestyle options and can become a marker for exploring the nature and local politics of cultural diversity. Wayne Swan has used this signifier accordingly to compare one neighbourhood with another for the sake of showing how in a global economy Australia has become a patchwork quilt of winner and losers.[2]

The prospect of a theological employment of postal-codes will seem most unusual at first glance. Its practice relies on the now well recognized turn to cultural analysis and criticism in theology. In her description of this cross-disciplinary work, Sheila Greeve Davaney has identified two "accompanying innovations." The first is a concern with "ordinary people and their everyday lives and practices." The turn is towards a popular view of culture and, by way of extension, a second interest in the "material practices and dimensions of religions." The tendency of this turn of cultural analysis is to be less satisfied with theological ideas as "disembodied abstractions" that possess "ghostly lives." Even the theologian is now called upon to furnish some sense of identity and an explanation of social location.[3]

The postal-code option directs attention towards named and numbered environments. It opens up the possibility of a localized theology that engages with the icons of belief and value, and the call to mission, that are embedded in the experiences of Will Storrar's notion of "neighbourhood saints." The postal-code allows theology to go glocal. From this vantage point Christian identity is a global flow that is both catholic and yet very specific and earthed in the public life of the strangers, the neighbours and the "cohabiting citizens" with whom we rub shoulders in the acting out of our daily lives.

The invitation the postal-code offers theology is for faith to take seriously the question concerning who is our neighbour and to do so for Christ's sake. It puts the possibility of human faces before us and lays upon

---

2. Swan, *Postcode*.

3. Davaney, "Theology and the Turn to Cultural Analysis."

the discipline the imperative of making room for what Rebecca Chopp has described as a "poetics of testimony."[4] Here the focus is upon a "discursive practice" of telling tales that reveal truth as it is experienced by individual selves and "what [that] truth [then] means to [their] communities." It is more like a "vow" or a "promise" to say what has happened rather than a desire to formulate an abstract theory or statement. It is subjective and yet the very nature of testimony also blurs the boundaries between the personal and the public. It is about bearing witness, and, in Chopp's opinion, the telling of these stories is for the mending of life and invoking a moral claim. Now such discourse is suggestive most obviously of interrogation and the courtroom but Chopp reminds us that testimony and witness also lie at the heart of the Christian reading of the existential significance of Jesus. For the sake of a theology that is bound to postal-codes this poetics enables the practice of this discipline to put a human face upon the local neighbourhood.

For us living at the ends of the earth, Dutney's analogy of the postal-mark puts the case for a localized theology responsive our life on the map. The postal-code reference invites us to be more specific with respect to the *habitus* in which we perform this task. And Chopp's poetics of witness is consistent with the method recently adopted by the social scientist, Anthony Moran, in his study of the Australian experience of globalization.[5] In this instance Moran made the case for a balance between the theoretically informed debates on what constitutes globalization witness a series of personal narratives that witness to the changes that have engulfed Australia, often under the rubric of "opening up," "reinventing" and "remaking." Such stories put "everyday experience to the forefront" and, so Moran argues, "bring the [dense theoretical] debates to life."

The importance of this latter step in the argument cannot be underestimated. The setting in which theology in Australia is done is now much changed. The well-established global flows of feminism, liberation, human rights and ecological concern are now placed alongside a raft of diasporic and cross-cultural issues. Moran's interest lies in what constitutes national belonging and identity, whether multiculturalism should be seen as a threat or an opportunity, the dilemma of settler/indigenous relations and the politics that surround asylum seekers. In such a changed location Charles Sherlock has observed how the God images prevalent in Australian society have

---

4. Chopp, "Theology and the Poetics of Testimony."
5. Moran, *Australia*.

moved over several decades from the relative stability of a transcendent God being like "the bloke upstairs" to more immanental model of a spirituality sponsor.[6] In a way that could not have been foreseen Andrew Hamilton has also wondered whether it is possible to do theology any longer in Australia after Woomera—this postal-code being an icon of detention and the silencing of voice through the sewing together of lips.[7] The theological task has become even more complex in the wake of 9/11, the Bali bombings and the recent explosions on the London tube. *Terra Australis* has become *terror Australis*.[8]

Our urban neighbourhoods have radically changed in a relatively short period of time. Islam is now in our backyard. The more homogeneous world of an Anglo-Celtic Australia and who is one of us has given way to the rhetoric and practice of multiculturalism. The literature testifies to the possibility of being alter/asian, Arab-Australian, hyphenated and hybrid and even Australienated. The imperative for a theology that is directed towards the concrete realities of our life here and now could scarcely be more pressing.

NSW 2117, 2150, 2151

Let me be more particular. The postal-codes which form the environment in which I do theology have to do with residence, work, worship and consumption. My home lies inside NSW 2117. Where I live is the demographic heart of Sydney, though the Harbour Bridge, the coat-hanger, can only be seen from the top of the highest hill. This postal-code lies close to the end of the navigable part of the Parramatta River where colonists and convicts from the north settled on aboriginal land. Out of my dining room window there are the rising edifices of Sydney's principal secondary commercial centre and its intersection with a bevy of transnational companies. This is NSW 2150. At its consumer heart lies the expansive Westfield mall and its international food court. Out of my study window I can see the Olympic Stadium, a global icon for a couple of weeks in the millennial year of 2000, and a cultural symbol for the role sport plays in the self-understanding of this country. This complex of superdomes and stadia of various designer-sizes is situated on the edge of Auburn where the nearest neighbours for

---

6. Sherlock, "From 'Mate Upstairs' to 'Spirituality Sponsor.'"
7. Hamilton, "'Theology after Woomera."
8. Pearson, "From *Terra Australis* to *Terror Australis*."

the local Tongan Christian congregation belong to the Turkish Ottoman-styled mosque. Further to the south east, out of my sight, lies Lakemba, nicknamed Lebkemba.

Back at 2117 my next door neighbour on one side is Greek and on the far side of them are the Indonesians. My other neighbour is from Hong Kong. Across the road are the Koreans, and to their right the Australian of Italian descent who is married to a Chinese woman from Shanghai. Vince and Carmel are "real Australians" who can remember when our crescent was developed. They have been stable residents; they have not left home in terms of their house but the level of change around them means that their neighbourhood is no longer the home site they remember.

The college where I teach belongs to an adjacent postal-code: 2151. The classroom is often awash with cultural diversity. It is committed to what is called a *communitas* programme designed to explore how, in living in the liminal spaces in between ethnicities, we engage in the art of forming new community The idea is taken from the theoretical work of Victor Turner and is replicated in the call to be a liturgical being.[9] The congregation where I worship is back at postal-code 2150. On the second Sunday evening of every month it undergoes a conversion. The staple diet of worship services gives way to a circle of friendship. The semiotics are of a different order. The primary focus is a meal and conversation, sometimes around a specified theme. The implicit theology is one of hospitality. Only a small to middling percentage of those who attend will have worshipped according to Christian convention earlier in the day. Those who come together now are from a range of cultures: Venezuela, Peru, Chile, Argentina, Uruguay, Tonga, Niue, China, Singapore, Korea, Turkey, Afghanistan, Iran, Iraq, Myanmar and the Congo. The event is inter-cultural and inter-faith.

NEIGHBOURS

These postalcodes signify neighbourhoods of an Australia that is being re-made in keeping with Moran's diagnosis. And yet there is a need for a word of caution lest a misleading impression is constructed. Moran himself is very careful to place his interviews and personal narratives with migrants alongside those of Kel and Mick who represent an older "true blue" type of Australian. With respect to the ethnic diversity found in my crescent these men "didn't have any exposure to those sorts of people." Their postal-codes

---

9. See Mitchell, "*Communitas* of Christ: Risking the Cross-Cultural Way."

are not like mine. It is more probable that a family tree, genealogy, plays as much a part in determining their identity as do their addresses. Their line of descent looks back to an earlier pattern of migration and settlement [or invasion] that was built upon the myth of Australia being *terra nullius* and which subsequently established the "core imaginary" of this society. Its self-understanding is of a relocated Anglo-Celtic identity. Its history is one of sharp definitions of who could be "one of us" and was mediated for the earlier part of the twentieth century through a discriminatory immigration policy based on race.

The presence of the "sort of people" my neighbours are was made possible by the dismantling of a corpus of restrictive legislation. Gwenda Tavan has described the origins and purpose of such policy, its administration and dependence on a particular style of bureaucracy, and how it was modified along the way in response to a changing world-order and the dictates of trade and the image being presented abroad. The opening up of Australia to peoples from anywhere and everywhere can be signpostaled as one of the achievements of the short-lived Labour Government of Gough Whitlam, 1972–1974, but even now it is not without its critics. Was it the work of a political and bureaucratic elite? Was it foisted upon an unsuspecting nation? Were its implications for work and national identity and citizenship sufficiently thought through?[10]

Those "true blue" Australians Moran interviewed were not opposed to the "newcomers" from a wider world who arrived as a consequence. The occasional outburst of anti-Asian sentiment and "paranoid nationalism" described by Ghassan Hage should be set alongside the widespread conviction that Australia is now a multicultural society. Exactly what that claim might mean and whether the models of social construction it releases are the most appropriate is far from self-evident. It is a "contentious, still evolving theme."[11] And yet the word itself has, nevertheless, become a fixture in the "national lexicon" and "virtually a household term in the public discourse" of Australia.

There is a balancing or compensating rhetoric that is often placed alongside this rather ready usage of the multicultural neologism. The invitation to be a "real Australian" can almost be like an altar-call and is closely associated with the possibility of something being "unAustralian." The politics of this kind of language has been subject to the most searing critique by

---

10. Tavan, *The Long, Slow Death of White Australia*.
11. Rothwell, "Our Way to Greater Harmony."

Hage. These fundamental values are reckoned to be at times contradictory, dependent upon a selective reading of Australian history and not necessarily peculiarly Australian at all.[12] For all the merits of this deconstruction the language remains. It is a signpostal pointing towards some unease as to how the neighbourhood has changed and implies that the best way ahead is one of assimilation and integration. Those who have come later should adapt to the law and customs and the expectations, more or less, of the core Anglo-Celtic identity already negotiated in a land down under.

For Miriam Dixon the function of this core is to be a "holding centre." The present is a "transitional period" during which time a "poly-ethnic nation" displaces the ethnic nation. In her concern for the imaginary Australian society Dixon argues that this core culture must play a key cohesive role. Its vocation is to privilege "those influences making for a social coherence which works at a satisfactory day-to-day level." The focus for Dixon is on that which integrates a nation. The fear is of fragmentation, the loss of civic identity and the emergence of a surface self that lacks emotional depth and commitment to the community at large other than which is bestowed by an institutional framework. For the sake of this transition Dixon believes that it is crucial that a positive sense of being Anglo-Celt, of being core, be reclaimed, though she is not blind to its defects. Nor is she unaware of the benefits that might accrue to the "Australia of the future" from living with "this astonishing new degree of difference." The present is a "period of consolidation" and a core culture "imparting its steadying sameness and cohesion to institutional patterns and broad values."[13]

The presence of this line of thinking is there for all to see. The character of my postal-codes is a far-cry from the fictive coastal towns and suburbs that litter Australia television soaps like *Neighbours*, *Home and Away* and now the comic *Kath and Kim*. In those imaginary worlds the neighbours belong to the relatively likeminded *cul-de-sac* (Ramsay Street), satirized suburbs (Fountain Lakes) and small seaside towns (Summer Bay). The cast of characters in each one of them is not noted for its cultural diversity. The turnover of attractive younger people is kept in balance by maintaining a stable, older, regular crew who represent the racial composition of Moran's more homogeneous Australia. In the opinion of Derek Weber the serial scripts of this distinctive genre create virtual communities

---

12. Hage, *Against Paranoid Nationalism*, 69–78.
13. Dixson, *The Imaginary Australian*, 1–11.

of meaning within a fast-paced, changing wider real-time society.[14] In this instance these popular soaps are essentially conservative. They mediate a kind of nostalgia. Their focus on suburban and beach cultures respectively is consistent with a well-established tendency in the study of how an Australian identity has been constructed.[15]

FAITH IN A HYPHEN

This theory of a holding centre sits rather uneasily with the emerging cultural turn in theology. The impression sometimes entertained that a more overtly contextual theology can collapse faith into a form of civic religion or an ideological prop for a vested interested is misleading. The very nature of theology presupposes a desire to find a point of transcendence that can stand at a remove from the presenting culture. That dialectic is embodied in the stock question that has shaped so much such theology: "Who is Jesus Christ for us today?" The necessity of defining who this "us" is and how one manages the hermeneutics of "today" can become consuming, but the legacy of Dietrich Bonhoeffer remains. The first word is "who," and this "who" signifies the presence (or absence) of the one who is always a stranger to us and who lies beyond our cultural captivities and holding centres.

The postal-mark analogy invoked by Dutney was designed to respect that being "in Christ" and also construct a theology that was more directly addressed to life in Australia. The underlying intention was soteriological. It was specific rather than generic. What is it about the human condition as it is lived out in this particular place, by this particular people, at this time that requires the healing, wholeness, reconciliation, and forgiveness that is mediated in and through the Christ event? The purpose was redemptive.

The difficulty with Dutney's analogy was one of timing. It was tied to a recognition of two centuries of settlement that had born witness to the history of this core culture. In theological terms its intention was to encourage an Australian theology that would not imitate the cultural cringe of yesteryear and simply replicate what had been done on the other side of the globe. The dilemma was that this Australia was rapidly changing. Would the practice of theology take sufficiently into account the escalating levels of cultural diversity and complexity? Would it address matters of diaspora,

14. Weber, "Everybody Needs Good Neighbours."
15. See Huntsman, *Sand in Our Souls*; also O'Hanlon, "Cities, Suburbs and Communities."

hybridity and hyphenation, and develop a theology of engaging with the ethnic and the religious other? Would it indeed allow a wider range of theological voices from within its own midst to break silence and express a cultural perspective in a first language that was not English? What if more faith was put in a hyphen that acknowledged the lines of continuity and discontinuity between a broad range of sending cultures and the national site of a receiving Australia?

Dutney's analogy lay at the end of one stage and on the threshold of another. The present concern for postal-codes, neighbourhood saints and the poetics of testimony represent a way of reading the "us" which is more differentiated. It forces the practical theologian to attend to what is there in front of us. The familiar metaphor of being "down under" might even then take on a new lease of life and become a tool of cultural criticism. No longer is its purpose merely to carry on a kind of banter between Australia and the United Kingdom which has its origins in imperial history. Nor need the metaphor refer to a cartographic site and fulfil a function equivalent to how the Far East is named. Now the imagery of being down under is more perspectival and suggests a hermeneutic of exploring faith from the underside and not just in the categories of what is core and a holding centre that exercises stability.[16]

Such a line of interpretation is most apposite for a theology that is grounded in the kind of postal-codes I know. It is a not uncommon for those who have migrated from radically different societies to feel at a disadvantage and consider themselves to be on the margins. The idea of a poetics of witness presupposes that there is a body of knowledge which, in this instance, knows from subjective experience how migration is always an act of dislocation. The hyphen represents both that rupture and the hope of a better life, variously construed.

HOME AND AWAY

Living in diaspora is almost always a more complex business than those who constitute Dixson's holding centre realize. There is a loss of place, status, markers of identity and a fundamental break in personal narrative. There is frequently felt an inner pressure to invent a new sense of identity and also construct a new sociality. The tendency is towards a deterritorializing of the self and a process of detraditonalizing. For those who inhabit

16. See Pearson, "For Christ's Sake."

these liminal spaces the most searching questions can become, where is home? and, who are we?

How to map this space and develop an explorers' hermeneutic lends itself to the autobiographical. An example of such is the writing of Sisilia Tupou-Thomas, a Tongan woman living in Sydney courtesy of Auckland. She describes herself as a "drifting seed," "an Australien," who is "out of place and out of time." She no longer fits in easily with the hierarchical island society she left thirty years before and which, once upon a time, was home. Who am I? Where am I now? Why am I here and not there? These have become her away positioning questions.[17]

The prospect of developing a diasporic theology emerging out of these experiences has become a contextual imperative. For those who study theology at NSW 2151 this task has acquired a certain momentum. It is recognized that this discipline must now make room for those who inhabit the spaces in-between two or more cultures and attend to how those spaces are negotiated through differences in gender and generations. In this instance the cultural turn in theology and Chopp's poetics cannot but help privilege the knot of issues to do with identity that Tupou-Thomas has named. That discourse is never merely selfish and introspective. The very idea of identity assumes the practice of relationship and encounter with the other. For the construction of a diasporic theology the work that is done within a particular culture cannot readily rest satisfied with how that faith is being understood and maybe revised within the confines of that "home." The highly heterogeneous nature of our postal-codes means that even within one faith there is a mixing of ethnicities and a possibility of a diasporic theology developing different emphases in another linguistic and ethnic community. Peter Phan has elsewhere named the need for a method that aspires after an inter-multicultural theology and which can an engage with the dominant culture.[18] And then there is that other nagging question that stalks diaspora. What happens when a migrant theology looks back over its shoulder away towards what was once home but is no longer?

The agenda that has surfaced for a theology that bears the postal-mark Australia is now richly textured. It has become peopled by an array of diverse neighbours finding their voice. The distinctive shape of these emergent diasporic theologies is determined by a threading together of three discrete threads that recognizes this dialectic. The critical question has to

---

17. Tupou-Thomas, "Telling Tales."
18. Phan, *Christianity with an Asian Face*, 11–25.

do with how being hyphenated is informed by a desire to weave in a concern for Christian identity as well. Who is Jesus Christ for us today, when that "us" is Tongan-Australia, Vietnamese-Australian, Korean-Australian or . . . ? This threading principle has then been interwoven with an imperative to relate to what is reckoned to be the core culture. Writing from within that settler centre, Jon Humphries has made the case for a theology of the cross and a cross-cultural hermeneutic to take the place of the more common ethos and politics of multiculturalism.[19] The underlying assumption is an Australian theology must make more room for those whose discipleship and confession has been moulded by a rather different experience of citizenship or cohabitation. For Seforosa Carroll the third strand is a Christology and an ethic of hospitality that frequently reverses the roles of guest and host. From her background in the Pacific she has used the analogy of the weaving of a frangipani *lei* as a symbol of welcome, embrace, flexibility and connectedness. The subversive function of this *lei* lies in how Carroll employs an alien custom for the sake of showing how a migrant culture can contribute to the way in which theology can be done in this *locus*.[20]

These theological initiatives better reflect the constituency of a globalized urban postal-code than do the casts found in those popular television soaps. For all its promise this reading of a diasporic theology is still insufficient. The local neighbourhood—like the wider society—is a peculiar mix of the secular and the multifaith. The metaphor of home and way equally applies to the faithful neighbour who is likewise the product of migration but whose faith happens to be different. In a climate of *terror Australis*, where matters of faith are inclined to be regarded a private affair in a public domain that prides itself on the virtue of tolerance, what kind of God-talk should be privileged? Can the contours of a Christian diasporic theology assist?

The sociological study that has been carried out the settlement of religions in Australia by Gary Bouma has shown that many of the basic practical matters of organizing a community of worship that serves a migrant minority are somewhat similar.[21] The same is true with respect to the search for identity and generational difference. There is scope here for an interfaith encounter that is less dogmatic and more a poetics of witness. And yet all is not equal. The dilemma that Hage and Abbas El-Zein has identified is

19. Humphries, "Crossing into the Unknown."
20. Carroll, "Strangers and Frangipani *Lei*."
21. Bouma, *Many Religions, All Australian*.

that Islam, for instance, is also perceived to be an alien faith and so stands in yet a more vulnerable space. Here the issue is not always one of where is home but whether the Muslim migrant can ever overcome the feeling of being no more than a guest and negotiate a way through competing cultural understandings of what is indeed meant by guest.[22] This dilemma has become intensified through the flow of global politics. What is it like to be Muslim, to be an Arab-Australian, in a time when the media abounds with headlines and special reports of radical Islamic cells, the naming of likely iconic targets, and the outlining of emergency evacuation procedures? All the while the world's most populous Muslim country lies to the north, the nearest neighbour.

GOING PUBLIC

Perhaps a diasporic theology can go public. It has the capacity to represent what it is like to inhabit a liminal space. It knows what it is like to be on the edge. Such a theology is well aware of the benefits of relationality and the complex dialectic of hospitality. The diasporic understanding of faith is built upon a quest for room being made for the would-be citizen who is, at first, an alien. It is time for a disaporic theology to go inter-faith and help create a less fearful set of public postal-codes.

---

22. El-Zein, "Being Elsewhere."

WORKS CITED

Bouma, G. D., editor. *Many Religions, All Australian: Religious Settlement, Identity and Cultural Diversity*. Melbourne: Christian Research Association, 1996.

Carroll, S. "Strangers and Frangipani *Lei*: Exploring a Christology of Hospitality." In *Faith in a Hyphen: Cross-Cultural Theology Down Under*, edited by C. Pearson, 145–58. Sydney: UTC Publications, 2004.

Chopp, R. "Theology and the Poetics of Testimony." In *Converging on Culture: Theologians in Dialogue with Cultural Analysis and Criticism*, edited by D. Brown et al., 56–70. The American Academy of Religion Reflection and Theory in the Study of Religion Series. Oxford: Oxford University Press, 2001.

Davaney, S. G. "Theology and the Turn to Cultural Analysis." In *Converging on Culture: Theologians in Dialogue with Cultural Analysis and Criticism*, edited by D. Brown et al., 3–16. The American Academy of Religion Reflection and Theory in the Study of Religion Series. Oxford: Oxford University Press, 2001.

Dixson, M. *The Imaginary Australian: Anglo-Celts and Identity, 1788 to the Present*. Sydney: UNSW Press, 1999.

Dutney, A. "Postal-mark Australia." In *From Here to Where? Australian Christians Owning the Past, Embracing the Future*, edited by A. Dutney, 1–9. Melbourne: Uniting Church Press, 1988.

El-Zein, A. "Being Elsewhere: On Longing and Belonging." In *Arab-Australians Today*, edited by G. Hage, 225–40. Carlton South: Melbourne University Press, 2002.

Hage, G. *Against Paranoid Nationalism: Searching for Hope in a Shrinking Society*. Annandale: Pluto, 2003.

Hamilton, A. "Theology after Woomera." In *Refugees: Justice or Compassion*. Special issue, *Interface* 5/2 (2002) 108–21.

Humphries, J. "Crossing into the Unknown." In *Faith in a Hyphen: Cross-Cultural Theology Down Under*, edited by C. Pearson, 159–74. Sydney: UTC Publications, 2004.

Huntsman, L. *Sand in Our Souls: The Beach in Australian History*. Carlton South: Melbourne University Press, 2001.

Mitchell, S. "*Communitas* of Christ: Risking the Cross-Cultural Way." In *Faith in a Hyphen: Cross-Cultural Theologies Down Under*, edited by C. Pearson, 174–85. Sydney: UTC Publications, 2004.

Moran, A. *Australia: Nation, Belonging, and Globalization*. New York: Routledge, 2005.

O'Hanlon, S. "Cities, Suburbs and Communities." In *Australia's History: Themes and Debates*, edited by M. Lyons and P. Russell, 172–89. Sydney: UNSW Press, 1989.

Pearson, C. "For Christ's Sake: From Expletive to Confession." *Pacifica* 17 (2004) 197–215.

———. "From *Terra Australis* to *Terror Australis*." *Eremos* 85 (2003) 8–11.

Phan, P. C. *Christianity with an Asian Face: Asian American Theology in the Making*. Maryknoll, NY: Orbis, 2003.

Rothwell, N. "Our Way to Greater Harmony." *The Weekend Australian*, 13 May 2002.

Sherlock, C. "From 'Mate Upstairs' to 'Spirituality Sponsor': God Images in Australian Society." In *Developing an Australian Theology*, edited by P. Malone, 43–64. Strathfield: St. Paul's, 1999.

Swan, W. *Postcode: The Splintering of a Nation*. North Melbourne: Pluto, 2005.

Tavan, G. *The Long, Slow Death of White Australia*. Melbourne: Scribe, 2005.

Tupou-Thomas, S. "Telling Tales." In *Faith in a Hyphen: Cross-Cultural Theology Down Under*, edited by C. Pearson, 1–4. Sydney: UTC Publications, 2004.

Weber, D. C. "Everybody Needs Good Neighbours: Soap Opera as Community of Meaning." In *Religion and the Media: An Introductory Reader*, edited by C. Arthur, 113–24. Cardiff: University of Wales Press, 1993.

2

Postal-Code 2016/2017
Redfern/Waterloo in South Sydney

Dorothy McCrae-McMahon

THIS ESSAY IS BEING written from the perspective of ministry through the South Sydney congregation of the Uniting Church in Australia. The ministry areas which it generally covers are the Sydney suburbs of Redfern and Waterloo.

According to the 2006 census, Redfern has a population of 11,483 people, with Indigenous people making up 2.4% of the population. 37.9% of the population was born overseas. English was primarily spoken at home by 55.9% of the population, with the most important other languages being the Chinese languages (5.5%), Russian (2.4%), Greek (2.4%), and Arabic (1.7%).[1] Twenty-five percent of the population identified with no religion/atheism, higher than the national average. Of the remainder, 19.9% were Catholic, 10.9% Anglican, 4.4% Eastern Orthodox, and 3.9% Buddhist. Furthermore, 41.6% of the population lived in public housing.

According to the 2006 census, Waterloo has a population of 11,122 people, with Indigenous people making up 3.4% of the population (higher

---

1. Some census data taken from Australian Bureau of Statistics, "2006 Census Quick Stats: Postal Area 2016. Released on October 25, 2007. Online: http://www.censusdata.abs.gov.au/.

than the national average). 43.3% of the population was born overseas. English was primarily spoken at home by 48.8% of the population, with the most important other languages being Chinese languages (10.0%), Russian (5.9%) and Indonesian (2.8%). The largest religions were Catholicism (22.4% of the population), Anglicanism (10.0%), Buddhism (5.7%) and Eastern Orthodoxy (3.7%). Furthermore, 19.7% of the population identified with no religion/atheism, slightly above the national average. Forty-seven percent of the population lived in public housing, and the unemployment rate was 16.6%, significantly higher than the national average.

There are several themes running through the lives of people here. One is racism against the Indigenous people of this land—people who now often struggle with poverty, addictions and many forms of abuse. Then there are non-Indigenous people who often suffer from mental illness, addictions and troubled histories, many of whom are homeless and gather around parks and streets in the area. Also, the significant areas of public housing are often occupied by older people of different ethnic groups who need various levels of support and encouragement.

Now interwoven with these groups are mostly youngish professionals who work in the nearby city, tertiary students attending several university campuses and a significant number of people from the gay, lesbian, bi-sexual and transgender community. Many of the young professionals and students were turned off the church in their youth, or come from families who had that experience. They cannot imagine finding Christianity relevant to their lives and yet may well contemplate activities like yoga or various forms of meditation and spirituality in general.

On the other hand, the GLBT community is filled with people who have been wounded and betrayed by the Christian church and other religions. Often they have had past connections with conservative or Pentecostal forms of the faith and, deep in their souls, they carry words like "abomination." Even mentions of "sin" often engage with dark and punishing images in their souls.

Listening and watching the people and churches in the area, I would suggest that there are four main theologies which are being offered to and engaged with by the people in this postal-code who connect with Christianity.

The first is related to the traditional theology and worship of the Orthodox churches in the area—mainly Greek and Coptic. I would not presume to describe these in detail, but would rather simply observe that

Orthodox theology usually rests securely and reassuringly within the Liturgy which is celebrated each week. There the people are embraced in the great Feast of Heaven—the tastes, touches, sounds and fragrance of incense which carry them into promises of what is to come. Because this Liturgy is, of its essence, corporate, the people come and go within it, confident that nothing rests on them alone but rather in the gathered people of God.

Given the neediness of so many people here, the second theology which initially seems popular is the one which offers a God who rewards those who join the faith with prosperity and success. Obviously, this can be very attractive to people with significant needs. It also gathers in many young people, at least for a while. They are invited in with promises of good and songs and bands which lift their hearts in hope. It feels good to be part of a large gathering, where they can meet other young people and be part of a church which seems to be very sure of what it believes.

They stay with this "uncomplicated" God for a while and then drift off because it becomes clear that, either this God doesn't love them because the rewards are not forthcoming, or this God is not true because life brings the hard questions. The Bible is placed at risk for them because their minds cannot live with its literal interpretations. Their faith is often endangered because, if their prayers are not answered and they challenge those teaching this theology, they are sometimes told that it is because they lack faith or they are sinning.

If they are Indigenous people, it is also often the same God who has been offered to people like themselves in the nineteenth and twentieth centuries missionary movements. It is interesting to note that the first conversion of an Indigenous person in the Australian colony took almost one hundred years—so foreign was the God offered in relation to the spirituality of the most ancient surviving community of people on the planet. This God was frequently a patronisingly simplistic God and rarely one which was taught with other than a literalistic view of the Bible. In many cases it was brought by the same people who participated in herding them into mission stations and sometimes became a theology of control.

When we look at the third theology present in Postal-code 2016/2017 it offers to those in need a kindly and generous God and to those who serve them, one who demands endless gifts to others with few questions attached. This encourages here whole groups of people who cluster around the outskirts of the churches, almost demanding a God who literally gives unquestioning donations of money and goods into their lives. This God, through the people of God, endlessly responds to begging hands and the accompanying often tall stories. Indeed, this God, through the people, feels guilty if the gifts are not given. This is especially present when the person asking for help is of Indigenous origin and those being asked to give are non-Indigenous.

The history of relationships bears the pain of the discrimination and injustices which have prevailed. This approach to God works well for quite a while in some places, but doesn't really invite life in either the givers or receivers—just anxiety or a sense of being endlessly needed in the first and often dependency and dishonesty in the second. It is also interesting to note that it rarely actually engages those asking for help with the life of the church and attendance at worship.

Most local churches who offer this God have histories of ministers, pastors and priests, together with congregations who have tried various approaches to both worship and faith with the people around them and who have brought this endlessly charitable God into the area. There will almost always have been a radical social justice leader who became quite famous in his (it always was "his") day and possibly rather contentious in relation to the hierarchy of his church. This person was often followed by a more conservative evangelical member of the clergy who often alienated the congregation. In all this, the theology presented moved around in time.

If the congregation found it hard to defend the radical clergy, I suspect it was sometimes because the theology presented was related to a God who believed in justice, but how this justice was to be administered and what sort of God stood behind it, was often not deeply discussed. It was more a sort of Godly ideology accompanied by fairly dry spirituality. The priest or minister was popular with the needy people because he delivered practical help and defended them in the church and political scene, but didn't necessarily deliver a broad and mature understanding of the faith. Having said all that, the charity offered and received gave people a sense of a loving God who grieved with them in their need.

The fourth theology is one which has developed in several churches, including the one in which I am a member—the South Sydney Uniting Church. In order to explore what I believe is now a powerful and affective approach to theology in our Postal-code, I will discuss the way we have approached it in our parish. Our parishioners are a mixture of struggling people from various ethnic backgrounds and a group of mostly professional people who have returned to the church after a couple of decades of pain and alienation. Their average age is around forty and some of them are homosexual or transgender.

Most people have been attracted back into the church after reading the free local monthly paper—a sixteen-page tabloid produced by the parish and delivered to twenty-two thousand households. While it carries a regular Faith Column, in the manner of a daily paper like the *Melbourne Age*, its major focus is on the building of community—celebrating survivals, encouraging inclusiveness, offering local news and views, challenging politicians and reviewing the arts in the area. In this fairly indirect manner, the church gives signals about the God whom it loves and serves and people then dare to enter its doors. We now have a steadily growing congregation.

If I mention the above, it is because the theology for our postal-code often needs to be offered subtly and gently. You never lay the gospel on the ground lightly in South Sydney. To do so would be to mock many members of its community, to tell them that the solutions to their lives are simple, or to present a Christ who hasn't really noticed what is going on.

We are constantly reminded that the newcomers are often testing every moment to see what sort of God is there. Those of us who sing along the old hymns with enjoyment and sometimes only vague attention to the familiar words are asked, when we break for coffee, to explain how we can sing "those words." The people read what they sing! They also mostly sing with all their hearts.

Of course, the written, responsive liturgy and its following Eucharist every Sunday, in itself tells them who our God is. Does this God make them feel terrible and guilty during the confession and pound them with the need for forgiveness? It takes a while and much care in the wording to invite a gentle grieving as we come before the holy God and remember our humanness. And the assurance of pardon must tell of a kindly God who understands and gathers them into loving arms.

Those who do the readings often do so as though they are privileged and I remember one man, whose life is rather struggling, doing so in a manner and voice which sounded and looked almost professional. I commented after the service and he said proudly that the priests at his school had taught him to speak up and lift your face to the people at regular intervals and he had never forgotten that. It was one of the few things which he believed that he does well.

You watch the faces during the homily and they are almost all listening attentively, critically and hopefully to every word. Do they dare trust this God? Is it safe to stay? Their attention is far removed from the all too often switching off which may happen in congregations which have been born and bred into the church and who, sadly, don't expect to be surprised! It comes from a people who are almost afraid to believe that God could be a safe companion, not to mention the church. Several of them ask the minister if he/she can give them a copy of the homily to study at home and they often ask penetrating questions about what is there.

We almost always have a shared response to the word where people are invited to say a word or phrase in relation to a question which arises from the homily and engage in a symbolic action. For example, on Trinity Sunday, we had three strips of cloth across the communion table—green for the creator with a bowl of leaves sitting on it, purple for the Christ with little purple crosses on a plate and red for the Holy Spirit with candles waiting on it. The people were asked to share which Person of God felt closest to them at the moment and to take the appropriate symbol and place it on the cloth or light a candle. They may also do this in silence if they wish. The sharing is deeply moving, even though it may simply be brief and we often laugh or cry together as the word reaches out to touch us.

Then, after we pray for ourselves and others, we move into the Eucharist and gather around the table in a circle together. Especially when they first join us, people often don't assume that they are worthy to join the circle and some of them wait a while before they are willing to do so. Their God is still somewhat to be feared and the bread and wine offered not to be taken for granted or risked if there is a price to be paid in particular beliefs, which are still sometimes lying in their souls in a threatening manner. I have never before experienced so often a Eucharistic moment when I see the participants looking with love at each other and holding the bread as though it is precious beyond telling. It does truly become the Body of Christ and the sacred circle of love.

Over morning tea and in the monthly bible studies, people ask the really tough questions of the church and our God. The faith that survives here is not a childish version (as distinct from child-like). It must be one which is grown-up—matured by the testing of life and honest responses to that. These questions arise as the roughly two types of members mingle after church. This is not a pietistic congregation, nor one which falsely smiles at others in the name of Jesus. They are able to be trusted with whoever comes. They receive each other with all their differences because most of them have suffered because they are in some way "different" and they hold each other as they journey on. They are gathered in whether they come once a year or every week or everything in between.

So, who is this God who survives well and comes to life among the people in Postal-code 2016/2017? This God is revealed in scriptures which are presented in a way which is deeply informed by current biblical scholarship. Every Sunday the person who brings the homily has read widely and wrestled deeply to discover the truth and the good news which lies within the set passages of the lectionary. This God emerges from the stories and witnessing of the ancient peoples of Israel and the New Testament followers of Jesus Christ. The truth, as best as it can be discovered, arises from within the inspiration of a living God, not one who was captured and defined thousands of years ago.

This God is best discovered in a non-literal view of scripture which would demand of us that we believe in slaves obeying their masters, women being unclean when they menstruate and homosexual people being abominations. We see, with sympathy, the earthquake devastation of Sodom and Gomorrah and the frightened people trying to name a scapegoat for what they interpreted as an offending of their God—who best to blame than someone who is different and didn't contribute to the survival of the tribe in procreation? We thread carefully and respectfully through the witness of the people of God who have tried in faith to tell of their experiences with this God and to hand on their interpretation of what that means in terms of who this God is and who they must be.

It is a God who receives from us, like the psalmists, the shouts of anger and cries of protest which we shout into the universes as we experience the struggle of life in our day, both personally and as a world. It is a God who listens with love to our questions, as in Job and Habakkuk, when we say, "Why do the good die and those who oppress the people live? And why are some people visited by pain, loss and trauma while others go free of that?" In a theology which doesn't pretend to have all the answers to the hard questions, we live with a God who says, "I am weeping with you and I know what you are going through because I have walked this way. I will be with you and that will be enough."

We then can celebrate a church which, as the Body of Christ, says "We will hold onto each other and our God will never leave us nor forsake us." With Habakkuk, we are able to sing "The fig tree will not blossom, the vine will not bear fruit . . . but we will rejoice in the name of our God, the God of our salvation who lifts our feet and carries us into the high places" (Hab 3:17–19).

We teach a God who says to the people of all ages, "When the going is hard, I am not punishing you. No more sacrifices are needed, even though you fail and stumble in all your humanness. Look, to convince you of that, I will be the sacrifice. You are forgiven and I need no lambs, pigeons, children or virgins (or, for that matter, homosexuals) to be burned to gain my approval."

We point to the other deep and powerful theology of the cross and the words of Jesus who says, "Come. Take up your cross and follow me." We celebrate in this the great, lived-out paradigm, which is the gift of Jesus Christ. This is the God who treads the ground of our life and walks steadfastly towards all the powers and authorities which would destroy or oppress the people. This God lives so strongly that this walking the way must be stopped because it challenges the ungodly forces of this world. But, the wonder is that, when these forces think they have destroyed the Christ, paradoxically, a greater Godly risen life is brought into being—one which we may share if we dare to live out small echoes of the same journey. It offers a far more profound theology of life than that which has to do with rewards and punishments or endless piety.

While God calls us to be the people who participate in love, generosity and justice, the offer to us all—both giver and receiver is always to a deeper and grander life. It is not about colluding with dependencies (unless the person concerned is truly incapacitated). It is always an invitation to move away from being a victim and to invite in each other a step by step journey into freedom. It is not about living a life of endless charity but to bring it into creative and healthy balances of self-respect, rest and recreation, laughter and commitment to others. Gifts to others are given for their own sake and are not manipulative.

This God is not just a God of good works but one who visits us as we pause and enter the sacred place of worship and sacraments. Our life in faith is not a lonely personal journey but one which is the offering of our particular gifts into the forming of the Body of Christ in our place. We are not Jesus Christ but unique and beautiful specks of life in the great continuum of human existence, stretching into the distance of eternity in the past and the future. It matters what we do, but we may never see the fruits of what we offer as it is joined with human and divine endeavour.

As we pray—knocking, asking and seeking—we will be given the gift of the Holy Spirit. That will be given in many differing forms. It may come in healing, comfort, inspiration, courage, endurance, guidance, supportive friends, wisdom—all that lies within the Spirit and waits for us to come in hope and faith. We may not determine what the answer will be as we are not God and life is far too complex for us to think that we know what is best.

We know a God who often comes to us in friend and stranger in unexpected ways if we will be open to that. Our hearts are lifted up as the creation itself gives gifts of life in its soaring mountains and surging seas, its birds flying free and the tiny life around our feet. As the people of the city, we sometimes find God in the grass that grows through a crack in the concrete, the smile on the face of a delighted child or an old person sitting on the side of the street. We may see it in the sky which hangs low over the city skyline and the sun which trickles through the density of its busy life.

As the bread and the wine of the Eucharist is broken and poured out before us, we believe that all may join the feast of life around the holy table of Jesus Christ. There is placed in our hands the eternal signs that our God shares everything we need with us and is present in our midst in ways which are both infinitely earthed and profound mystery. We look around at the faces of those gathered and there find the true communion of saints. We hold the elements in our hands with gratitude and reverence and see there the life of Christ who will enrich our lives in ways beyond our telling.

In all this, the God of postal-code 2016 and 2017 is one who invites us to be honest, ask our questions and grow up in the faith so that we do not need to form our ghettos of literalism or the absence of doubt which lies so dangerously in fundamentalism. This God is often found afresh on the margins of life where so many of our people in this area live. Ours is a God who stretches out beyond the boundaries of our horizons and ever calls us on towards a greater hope than we have ever known. This God laughs and cries with us and holds us in the hollow of a loving hand as we go.

3

Postal-Code 3000
Imagining Sacred Space

Simon Holt

INTRODUCTION

"A DAY IN TOWN." That's what my mother always called it; our occasional but routine pilgrimage into the heart of Melbourne. For me, it was the highlight of school holidays. It meant a 50-minute train journey from my outer suburban home in Dandenong. Given how rarely I rode a train as a boy, this only added to the sense of intrigue. As our string of red carriages careered along the track, I watched—my nose pressed up against the window and my breath forming patterns on the glass—as the landscape slowly changed. The lines of perfectly spaced 1960s cream brick veneers, all with matching front fences and appended garages, gradually gave way to factories, graffitied walls and ever smaller back yards tucked behind late nineteenth century terraces. As the intensity of the residential landscape increased, so too did my fascination.

As we emerged from the platforms of Flinders Street Station, the hub of the city's rail network, we entered another world. Navigating the ticket barriers in the arrival hall, we moved from the shadows of the domed space into the daylight beyond and stood together under the clocks that kept time for departing trains. As my mother ensured that every member of the brood was accounted for, I dodged the stream of commuters brushing past to look out on the intersection below. With Young & Jackson's Hotel on one corner and the spires of St. Paul's Cathedral on the other, this junction was more alive than anywhere else I knew. The constant sound of car horns mingled with the clang of the trams that rattled by. An eternally replenishing pool of pedestrians gathered at the corner ready for their turn to cross Flinders and disperse into the anonymity of the city grid beyond.

Taking our place at the corner, we would cross with the mid-morning hordes and continue up the main artery of Swanston. My most enduring boyhood memory of the city is of suits, briefcases and umbrellas; a place of heels, hats and handbags. Everybody was on the move, many who looked as though they belonged. Important and self-assured people, they moved with purpose and an urbane indifference to everyone around them. There were those, too, who looked anything but important, disgruntled and dishevelled in fact, but equally at home, standing at corners with half-empty bottles or crouched on the ground with crumpled blankets by their sides. And then there were the boys who spruiked newspapers on every corner. Though they looked barely older than me, I assumed they knew the ways of this world better than I ever could.

We passed the city square and the Town Hall with its grand clock tower, the streets lined with buildings that rose endlessly toward the sky. Bourke Street was our initial destination with the Myer Department Store at its heart. First was our visit to the sixth-floor toy department followed by lunch in the cafeteria. I remember pushing my tray along the run, mesmerized by the lurid red and green jellies set in tall parfait glasses. Topped with whipped cream and glace cherries, they made lunch feel like a carnival. I remember window shopping in the Royal Arcade, lingering outside the Houpton Tearooms where beautifully dressed women from Camberwell sipped tea, and watching the private school boys rowing on the Yarra. I remember our mandatory visit to the Bible Society bookshop in Flinders Lane, and of course, the underground toilets on Elizabeth. An elderly attendant always stood in a corner, a dark room of supplies behind him and a mop at the ready. It was all very subterranean ... and very Melbourne.

I looked forward to our "day in town" all term. The city was a place in which I felt markedly my lack of sophistication and yet where life and possibility seemed endless. For me, it was a place of fantasy, one in which

I imagined myself as more at home than anywhere else. I determined then that one day I would belong to this place, and it would belong to me.

Today this city is my home. For the past nine years I have lived with my family within the boundaries of the City of Melbourne, three of those in a high-rise apartment in the CBD (Central Business District), postal-code 3000. Indeed, I do belong to this place, but I cannot claim it belongs to me.

Postal-code 3000 is an easily defined space built on a parcel of land "purchased" in 1835 by a Tasmanian opportunist John Batman. The unsuspecting "vendors" were the local Duttigalla Aborigines. The price: a collection of scissors, beads and blankets and the promise of a yearly rent of similar kind. Soon after, in 1837, two government surveyors, Hoddle and Russell, were charged with the task of laying out the form of this new settlement. What they devised was an intimate but tightly ordered grid of streets that sets the boundaries for postal-code 3000 today. This mix of broad tree-lined boulevards, narrow streets and an interconnecting web of laneways takes up no more than 1.5 square kilometeres yet has been the heart of the wider metropolitan region for more than 180 years.

AN IMAGINED LANDSCAPE; A CONTESTED SPACE

Postal-code 3000 is a very real place, tangible and concrete; one that daily plays host to around 800,000 people: residents, workers and visitors.[1] It is a centre of finance, commerce, government and education. It's a place of tall buildings, wide streets and narrow laneways; home to churches, courts and libraries. It is endless arcades of shops, sidewalk cafes, galleries and five star hotels. It is a place that you can see, feel, hear and smell. But it is more. As my childhood memories attest, the city of Melbourne is an imagined landscape, a place of fantasy in which its inhabitants, routinely or momentarily, re-imagine themselves. Though as a landscape of the imagination postal-code 3000 is much less tangible, it is just as real.

A corporate executive drives into the city from the domestic and mundane obligations of his suburban home. After ascending in the elevator to his office high above, he stands at his window and surveys the city spread out below. As he does, he daily re-imagines himself as a person of power, position and influence.

An international student arrives in the city from a far away land, leaving behind family but bearing their hopes and expectations. This city is

1. Silk and Bell, "Melbourne City User Estimates and Forecasts, 2004–2020."

a place that embodies the uniquely Western versions of opportunity and freedom, a place to access education, prosperity and new beginnings. In the city he re-imagines his future and himself.

A city resident, an empty nester who moved into her penthouse after raising a family in a more suburban place, entertains friends on her balcony overlooking the riverside marina. As she sips her champagne, the lights of the city skyline dancing behind her, she re-imagines herself as an urban sophisticate with the trappings of culture and success at her fingertips.

A middle-aged couple, tourists from overseas, come to this exotic urban landscape to photograph its vistas, imbibe its culture and purchase an experience of transcendence and difference. They do not come in search of the ordinary, but of cultural diversity, energy and otherness.

A suburban homemaker travels into the city for a day of shopping. As she wanders the laneway boutiques and grand department stores, she is happily distracted by the alluring promises of glamour. In every purchase, she re-imagines herself as a woman of style, noticed and desirable. Or perhaps she comes to enjoy the feast of concerts, theatres and restaurants—a momentary escape from an otherwise predictable domestic routine.

A young man from the outer suburbs invests considerable time re-making himself as masculine and virile. He primps and preens, gels and sprays before travelling with his mates into the city for a night of drinking, dancing and, if he's lucky, passion. For him, the city is a land of promise, an imagined place of transition from childlike constraint to the freedom of young adulthood.

From every perspective, the imaginative power of this landscape runs deep. Yet these imaginations, these competing visions of urban promise, are what make postal-code 3000 a highly contested space. One does not have to participate in its life for very long to feel the consequences. Overwhelmingly, the city's diverse constituencies envision themselves as adversaries competing for priority, space and resources.

Not long ago, I was invited to participate in a community forum at the Town Hall on the administration of liquor licenses. In recent years the city has struggled with increasing levels of alcohol-fuelled violence on its streets and the reputation that goes with it. There to represent the interests of residents, I was seated alongside licensees, community service and law enforcement personnel, representatives of retail and cultural associations, business leaders and elected members of local government. What ensued was a heated and ultimately fruitless clash of imaginations. More regular participation in the City's advisory committee on children and families only casts the divides in greater relief. Multiple proposals come before Council vying for the affirmation of Melbourne as an international city, a residential city, a 24-hour city, a city of literature and the arts, a child-friendly city, a world-class city of fashion and food, and more. Yet each proposal carries with it an implicit critique of competing visions for postal-code 3000.

As a city resident and as a Christian, I am compelled by the gospel call of Jesus to ask what part the church and I can play in this contested space. In his context, Archbishop of Canterbury Rowan Williams warns the urban church against becoming nothing more than one interest group among many bidding competitively for the same resources, recognition and priority that every other interest group seeks. According to Williams, the church is operating most closely to its vocational identity when is provides a "radically different imaginative landscape," one in which all constituencies can discover an alternative way of being and sharing life.[2]

Herein lies a word of vocation for people like me and for the faith communities that inhabit postal-code 3000. The city church is ideally placed to model a way of being in community that is genuinely inclusive and hospitable, a community of presence that can facilitate what Williams describes as "a conversion of sorts, a turning around of values and priorities that grow from trust in God."[3] Rather than settling to be an interest group cradling its own agenda, the church by its nature has the capacity to provide a radically different imagining, one of community, hospitality and cooperation. In doing so, perhaps the church can be part of enabling a gradual transformation of the urban landscape from contested space to something more genuinely human, inclusive and life-affirming.

FROM CONTESTED SPACE TO SACRED SPACE

The respected proponent of public spirituality, Philip Sheldrake, argues that the urban environment has a formative impact upon the human spirit. Places like postal-code 3000 shape the soul. City making, he says, is about the functional, the ethical and the spiritual. Good cities, cities that nurture the individual and collective spirit, are those that (i) enable the human person to flourish through the stages of life; (ii) nurture belongingness and connection; (iii) facilitate relationship with natural environments; and (iv)

2. Williams, "Urbanization, the Christian Church and the Human Project," 17.
3. Ibid.

offer access to the sacred or relate us to life as sacred.[4] It is this idea of the city as a facilitator of the sacred, an environment that potentially relates us to life as an integrated whole that may well provide a renewed sense of the church's place and purpose in the city.

In a contested space, the preferred narrative of arbitration centres on the notion of tolerance, "the catchword of liberal societies."[5] Tolerance carries with it a sense of forbearance, endurance or indulgence. In essence, it allows the "other" to be. A tolerant society is indeed a worthy aspiration; it stands in sharp contrast to a parochial and bigoted community intolerant of difference. But the word tolerant falls well short of describing the nature of sacred space and, within it, a community able to celebrate both its differences and common identity.

Sacred space is hospitable space. This more challenging notion of hospitality lies at the heart of the church's identity and mission. Henri Nouwen has described this mission as offering "an open and hospitable space where strangers can cast of their strangeness and become our fellow human beings." Such open sharing of space and place carries with it an obligation of surrender. Those in power and possession must be willing to relinquish ownership and allow others to fully inhabit space with them. My colleague Mark G. Brett writes of the need for a "divine counter empire of kenotic hospitality,"[6] a hospitality of surrender and self-emptying; one that enables a genuine sharing of space and resources and a much more profound expression of community. It is a costly business for it requires a giving away of self-interest in the interest of others

How might the church in postal-code 3000, through the expression of hospitality, facilitate such an opening up of the city as sacred space? I offer three limited suggestions.

HOSTING CONVERSATIONAL SPACE

Melbourne has its share of grand ecclesial buildings. Every Good Friday, I join thousands of others who make the pilgrimage of the cross from station to station around the streets of the city; from St Francis to St Paul's, from St Patricks to Scots Presbyterian and the grand white columns of Collins Street Baptist. There is much that can be critiqued, and often is, about the

---

4. Sheldrake, "Cities and Human Community," 108–9.
5. Ibid.
6. Brett, *Decolonizing God,* 184–85.

presence of such buildings, their "dwindling congregations," the never ending costs of maintenance and the sheer monetary value of the real estate upon which they stand. I have often wondered, though, what the city would be like if all of these structures were razed. What would be lost? Due to the sheer force of economics they would be replaced, no doubt, with yet more towers of glass and steal that pay homage to the powers of commerce and profit. But in the process something of the city's heart would be gone. Even among those who never darken the doors of such buildings, their presence is routinely affirmed. If nothing else, such buildings remind us of an alternative set of values, of possibilities that lie beyond the cold and rational dictums of the marketplace. Their dramatic spires point not to the glory of human industry, but to a reality beyond and to the sacredness of life itself, even in the city's urban heart.

In large part, the movement from contested space to sacred space depends on the power of conversation around values that bind us together; values that prioritize the dignity of humanity and community. In my view, the city church is uniquely placed to host and facilitate such conversations, inhabiting a space that is neither commercial nor public, neither partisan nor civic, but a space of genuine and open hospitality. For a church to take on such a role, to open its doors to conversations which are not explicitly religious in nature and which it cannot necessarily control, requires an element of self-emptying. To play the role of host is an act of intentional vulnerability, but one that has the capacity to impact well beyond the walls of the church building.

NURTURING LOCAL CONNECTIONS

In recent years, much has been said about the complexity of our place-identity and its importance to individual and collective wellbeing. This identity, especially for urban dwellers, is multi-faceted, a complex mix of the most local, micro-place connections of home and neighbourhood and macro-place relations to a wider, sometimes global, sense of place. For city residents, moving contested space into sacred space has to do with nurturing both connections.

Residential life in postal-code 3000 is unique. To those who look on from a suburban distance, it is a style of life easily caricatured, sometimes glamorized and commonly misunderstood. Today Melbourne's CBD is home to some 18,000 people, an increase of no less than 11,000 in the last six years. By 2031, the residential population is projected to be close to forty thousand people.[7] Given that in the early 1980s, there were a mere 700 people who called the city home, the growth in residential life is nothing short of extraordinary.

As in any residential context, city living can be an anonymous business. The majority of residents live in "vertical neighbourhoods," tall residential buildings that may be home to hundreds of individual households. More often than not, these residents have a strong sense of global identity. Their identification with the city as a whole is strong. As they look out of their living room windows or stand on their balconies, the perspective is broad, their sense of space defined by distant horizons and surrounded by towers of global industry. What's more, 42 percent of the city's population speak a language other than English in their homes. The more pressing challenge for city residents is the nurturing of those micro-place connections, connections to the immediate neighbourhood. Lacking some of the shared and contained spaces that define suburban communities—places such as schools, cul-de-sacs and corner stores—urban neighbourhoods need a stronger sense of local space and neighbourhood institution to thrive.

The churches of postal-code 3000 have always played an important role within their wider denominational traditions, "cathedral" churches with a central identity and a unique relationship to the wider metropolitan region. With the rebirth of the city centre as a lived-in community, and one that anticipates continuing growth, the city churches are faced with an extraordinary opportunity. By rediscovering their local parish identity, churches can play a significant role in the re-birthing of local neighbourhood. Doing so will require a considerable degree of surrender on the part of these churches. Self-identity runs deep. To embrace the immediate and local expression of their life may require their more regional identity to take a back seat for a while. But the commitment to hospitality, of the most practical and immediate kind, may well be its own reward.

MODELLING PRACTICAL INCLUSION

In the past few months, the plight of Indian students who come to Melbourne seeking skills, qualifications and the possibility of long-term residency has had a high profile in the media. The incidences of racial vilification, workplace exploitation and the inadequacy of educational programs set up to

7. Casey, "Analysis of Population and Housing 2001–2007."

profit from their aspirations has caused considerable debate. This has only piggy-backed on the wider story of tertiary education in Melbourne and the extraordinarily high number of international students, primarily from Asia, who call the city home.

In the past seven years, thirty-one apartment blocks have been built on the northern fringe of the CBD (between RMIT and University of Melbourne), the majority along Swanston Street. These apartments are now home to nearly ten thousand students, 95 percent from overseas. On a broader scale, the City of Melbourne is home to some twenty-five thousand international students.[8] In a research project conducted by the University of Melbourne, it was found that these students rarely make friends with Australians and commonly will never see the inside of an Australian person's home. Most often, they will live alone in very small rooms found for them by overseas agents. Furthermore, if they have them, their roommates will be other international students.[9]

All too often, the voices of such people go unheard in the public forums and conversations about city life. Though their presence adds a richness of life and diversity to the city landscape, they are not considered full participants. Most never have a vote, struggle with barriers of language and culture, are routinely exploited by opportunists and at the receiving end of passive racism and discrimination.

Though these students are just one group that sits on the margins of life in postal-code 3000, they represent a very tangible opportunity to the church. What other city-based communities are as well set up as the churches to provide space, support and intercultural relationships to these young people? It is often said that the transient nature of the international community makes serious investment in its welfare an act of no permanent gain for the church. But if the church is to play a key role in the movement of the city from contested space to sacred space, it has the opportunity to model a form of life that is genuinely hospitable, that seeks nothing in return and is willing to surrender its own comfort for the sake of others. Perhaps in so doing, the church can show the way, a different way, to the city as a whole.

---

8. Casey, "City of Melbourne 2006 Student Demographic Profile."
9. Morton, "Foreign Students Living on the Edge of Society," 4.

CONCLUSION

I have argued that postal-code 3000 is a highly contested space, one of competing imaginations. In the movement of the city from contested space to sacred space—space that is affirming of our shared humanity and community—I have suggested that the church has a key role to play. Flowing out of its commitment to self-giving hospitality as the expression of its identity and mission, the church can (i) host conversational space in which constituencies can hear and be heard, (ii) nurture local connections through re-embracing its parish identity, and (iii) model practical inclusion that brings the marginal into the centre of its life and mission.

Personally, I remain deeply committed to the welfare of postal-code 3000. My boyhood experience of "a day in town" and the imagined sense of self that came with it has slowly morphed into a life in town and an imagined sense of what this city might become. My imagined self and my imagined home remain connected as a landscape of faith.

WORKS CITED

Brett, M. G. *Decolonizing God: The Bible and the Tides of Empire*. The Bible in the Modern World 16. Sheffield: Phoenix, 2008.

Casey, N. "Analysis of Population and Housing 2001–2007." Melbourne: City of Melbourne, 2008.

———. "City of Melbourne 2006 Student Demographic Profile." Melbourne: City of Melbourne, 2008.

Morton, A. "Foreign Students Living on the Edge of Society: Towers of Segregation on CBD Fringe." *The Age*, 5 May 2007, 4.

Sheldrake, P. "Cities and Human Community: Spirituality and the Urban." *The Way* 45/4 (2006) 107–18.

Silk, B., and J.-A Bell. "Melbourne City User Estimates and Forecasts, 2004–2020." Melbourne: City of Melbourne, 2009.

Williams, R. "Urbanization, the Christian Church and the Human Project." In *Spirituality in the City*, edited by A. Walker, 10–18. London: SPCK, 2005.

4

Cross of Flowers
Echoes of Times Past or a Signpost toward a Future?

Matthew Wilson

It is the Easter long weekend. Outside the Uniting Church in postal-code 2079, on the Old Pacific Highway, stands a four-metre-high cross, covered in ivy, flowers, and ribbons. With the exception of one year, it has stood here for a few weeks every Easter for the last twenty-four years. Motorists heading home after a long weekend away snatch a glance at this slightly unusual and somewhat gaudy feature. Some heading north slow down and take a longer look. Locals walking past stop and comment that it looks good this year. There has never been a comment from the local council about the erection of this large, and obviously Christian, symbol on the side of a major road—but then the local State member of the NSW Parliament was, as usual, present when it was erected this year. The only year the flower cross was not put up it became a matter of letters to the local and major city papers. It has become an acceptable, quiet reminder of a Christian presence at Easter.

Postal-code 2079 is an outer suburb of Sydney. Sandwiched between National Park to the east, and State Recreation Reserves to the west, postal-code 2079 is stretched out along the ridge-lines, tendrils of housing pushing into the bushland around the Hawkesbury River catchment that defines the northern edge of Sydney. Apart from the bushland it is defined by three human-made features that have strongly influenced its development and the nature of its community. Along the main ridge-line heading north towards the river runs the old Pacific Highway—the former main Sydney-Brisbane route—for much of the last century the only road to the north of Sydney which did not rely on a ferry service. Closely following the road runs the main northern rail line. Finally, a little to the east of the old highway and the rail line runs the more recent scar of the Sydney-Newcastle Freeway. Extended through this area in 1988, it forms the eastern edge of the suburb, nestling alongside the Kuring-gai Chase National Park.

Originally known as Colah, what became postal-code 2079 began in the 1850s as a scattering of houses on the main road north out of Sydney. Originally a few houses, farms and orchards, its development really began with the coming of the Northern Railway in 1887.[1] The first church was built in the now renamed Mt Colah in 1919. It was a Methodist outpost of the Hornsby District. Like many of the buildings of the time it was a small weatherboard building—what today might be considered a "typical" Australian country church. In the post–World War II years, during the "baby boom," Mt Colah underwent its next major expansion. On the flat area to the east of the railway station alongside the National Park and along the Highway young couples bought land, built small fibro and weatherboard homes, and started families. Often tradesmen, or junior clerical workers they settled in this cheaper area to the north of the city. Many of these people form the older demographic of the suburb today. This period also saw the expansion of the church into the suburb—with the founding of small Anglican, Baptist, independent and Seventh-Day-Adventist congregations.

In the late 1970s and 1980s the improvement in building techniques and the need for affordable land on the transport corridor to the city saw a new wave of expansion, building and settlement. Housing estates extended out along the ridgelines pushing further into the State Recreation areas along Berowra Waters Creek to the west. Previously inaccessible battle-axe blocks on steep slopes were opened up, and the suburb more than doubled in size and population. These late "Boomers" did not build the small weatherboard and fibro homes of the post-war expansion. These homes were

---

1. The Northern Line opened from Sydney to Hornsby in 1886. The extension to the Hawkesbury River, including then Colah station was opened in 1887. In 1889 the "missing link," a rail bridge over the Hawkesbury and connecting line through to Gosford completed the Northern Line from Sydney Central through to Maitland and Newcastle, and then on to Brisbane.

modern timber and brick constructions, many designed to blend in with the bushland environment that had attracted their owners to the region in the first place. The socio-economic demographic had also changed. This wave of settlers was often young, university trained couples. Often children of senior professionals, they were moving into their own chosen professions. The land on the edge of the city was more affordable, but still within a fairly comfortable commuting time of work. This period also saw the decline of church attendance and the "neighbourhood church" leading to the closure of all but two of the Mt. Colah worshipping communities.

So, at Easter 2009 we have the current demographic of 2079. A postal-code with three distinct population bulges. The 1950s settlers, now well into their retirement with an increasing number of widows and widowers living on their own, the 1980s settlers, now heading towards retirement themselves, and their children, now in their teens and 20s, often still at home trying to find a career and affordable housing of their own.[2] Now another wave of change begins as a new generation of home-seekers succeed the 1950s settlers, replacing the weatherboard and fibro homes with townhouses or generic project homes, designed to fill the available block of land.

Stand at the foot of the Easter cross looking at the passing traffic, or conversing casually with the locals who pass, and you may form the impression of an educated, middle-class, Christian Anglo community. A community which likes to see itself as a stronghold of traditional Australian values—independence, mateship, a fair-go, keen on a "traditional" Aussie lifestyle—the bush and the water. Certainly the number of four-wheel drives and boats passing along the road, or Australian flags on flagpoles, hanging from rafters, verandahs or stuck in windows, letterboxes or car aerials might give you that impression, or the sunburnt blokes in blue singlets mowing their lawns. But spend a few moments at the Public School at pick-up time, or stand by the station steps and a radically different image of postal-code 2079 begins to emerge. You will be passed by girls and women

---

2. Demographic references are sourced from the Australian Bureau of Statistics Basic Community Profile 2079 from the 2006 Australian Census available from the ABS website: http://www.censusdata.abs.gov.au/ABSNavigation/prenav/ViewData?&action=404&documentproductno=POA2079&documenttype=Details&tabname=Details&areacode=POA2079&issue=2006&producttype=Community%20Profiles&-&producttype=Community%20Profiles&javascript=true&textversion=false&navmapdisplayed=true&breadcrumb=LPD&&collection=Census&period=2006&producttype=Community%20Profiles&#Basic%20Community%20Profile.

in Hijab or saris, men in turbans, Indians, Japanese, Malays, Indonesians, Filipinos, Burmese, Koreans, South Africans, Dutch. Like many Australian communities postal-code 2079 is changing, perhaps a little more slowly than in some areas, but then also, perhaps the denial of the cultural and ethnic change clings a little more strongly here—at least in the narrative identity of the suburb held by many of its residents.

In this moment of liminality, as the identity of the past gives way to a different understanding of what it is to be living in a northern commuter suburb of Sydney, Australia what does a flower cross by the side of the road represent to those who pass by? In a community which is becoming aware that the old meta-narrative of Australian identity somehow no longer fits reality, what does the church represent? Is the church a representative of the certainties of the past—a bastion standing stout in the face of a changing society, or is it a part of the change? Can the cross of flowers somehow provide a connection with daily experience? Can it say something about the changes and uncertainties encountered in daily life, or to an identity in flux? What opportunity does an Australian theology, an Australian church, an Australian Jesus have to speak to the heart of this particular community?

BEING AUSTRALIAN TODAY

Understanding, or even defining an Australian identity has never been as simple as is often assumed. Moran in his study of the Australian experience of globalisation noted the there were two stories of Australia—the first, following the thoughts of Kelly (2001)[3] he sees as portraying Australia up until the 1970s to 1980s as an insular Anglo settlement. The identity of this Australia was based on five "pillars"; namely the ideals of a White Australia, Industry Protection, Wage arbitration, state paternalism and imperial benevolence. The alternative Australia that Moran identifies sees the country as a homogenous and boring Anglomorph prior to opening to the rest of the world through industrial expansion and a major migration program following the Second World War, post-1945.[4] While the dating of the opening of Australia's self-identity from a monolithic Anglo culture may be debated, it is certain that until relatively recently this has been the core culture that has underlain the identity of Australia and Australians.

3. Kelly, "Labor and Globalisation."
4. Moran, *Australia*.

At a personal level, I can trace my descent through one line of the family to a somewhat suspect ménage à trois between the orphaned daughter of free-settlers to the colony of New South Wales who died on the outward journey from England with the Second Fleet in 1789 and a couple of freed English convicts. While these ancestors were pioneer settlers in rural New South Wales, my direct line of descent has been comfortably based in suburban Sydney for over 140 years. On the other side of the family both my grandparents were child migrants from Scotland and England to the north shore of Sydney immediately prior to and following World War I. While this fairly closely follows the common "Australian" anglo-celtic identity what does it say of those aspects of Australian identity which are often forgotten? As far as I know I can claim no indigenous heritage. Nor can I find links to other even more suppressed aspects of Australia's cultural, ethnic and religious heritage—the Chinese Buddhists of the 1850s gold rushes, the "Afghan" Muslim camel herders of the 1880s inland expansion, the Pacific Islander "Kanak" labour force. All these were major contributors to the building of Australia—even in the midst of this Anglo-White Australia that remained the core cultural sense of identity of the non-indigenous community.

Moran, along with many others,[5] also identify that the Australian mythological identity has also had a strong tendency to identify "country" or "bush" as the real Australia, while noting that in fact European Australia is, and always has been, a highly urbanised society. Evident in the nineteenth century stories of Henry Lawson and A. B. Patterson among others, it is an aspect of cultural identity that has remained strong, even as our major cities continue to grow as rural towns continue to age and shrink.

An echo of this ambiguous identity can be seen espoused by many in postal-code 2079. The bushland that surrounds the postal-code is highly valued by residents seeking an element of the "real" Australia while enjoying the convenience of being within a relatively easy commute of the Sydney central business district. Residents seek the advantages of the urban lifestyle, the ready access to employment, education, health services and amenities while also enjoying the proximity, and to a degree the illusion, of being adjacent to the "real" Australia. This ambiguity is enforced every summer as bushfires threaten residential properties and the risks of this proximity to the "real" Australia become more evident.

5. Moran, *Australia*. See also Mackay, *Advance Australia Where?*; and Elder, *Being Australian*.

Dixson, in her study of Australia's anglo-celitc identity identified that there have long been strong assimilationist trends within the core Australian cultural identity. She noted that often when talking about newer immigrants the phrase "should be mixing" should often be understood as meaning that "they" should be becoming like "us."[6] Hage suggests that the political shift towards a policy of multi-culturalism in Australia in the 1980s did not lead to the creation of a space where all Australians treat each other with respect and equality, but rather moved society towards a situation where the dominant cultural identity, the Anglo-Australian, agreed to tolerate other groups as long as they "behave."[7] Such cultural patterns tend to move us towards situations where minorities become invisible, and where the reality is not seen, because it does not conform to the notion of, as Dixson would state it "core identity." It becomes, in effect, a question of homogeneity versus diversity. In a place where ethnic, cultural, and increasingly religious diversity is the reality, how (or perhaps more pertinently why) do we seek to cling to a homogenous identity? Does our religious experience, and the local expression of church community, help or hinder the process of reshaping Australian identity?

Standing at the foot of the Easter cross we take a closer look. On close examination an interesting observation can be made. In this postal-code surrounded by Australian bushland, where many residents identify closeness to the Australian bush as one reason behind their choosing to live here, a startling omission soon becomes apparent. The flower cross is made of ivy. The flowers which create its visual impact are roses, delphiniums, dahlias—even a lotus blossom. In fact, on close inspection it becomes apparent that in the flower cross there are no native flowers or plants at all. In fact only the hardwood eucalypt posts that form the framework of the cross are indigenous to the environment in which it stands. The flower cross itself is, in its way, a symbolic representation of the community over which it stands. Built upon an indigenous base which few see, or even recognise is present, it is covered in flowering plants originating from various places around the globe—but predominantly the English country garden. Does it serve to remind those who see it that we form a community where, in reality, the vast majority of us are in some way "outsiders"? Is it a symbolic longing for the familiarity of the "old country"? Or is it a symbol of the

---

6. Dixson, *The Imaginary Australian*.
7. Hage, *White Nation*.

diversity of a new community built in this place, on the back of a strong, resilient, but often overlooked indigenous culture? Could it even be both?

PERSONAL FAITH, COMMUNITY VALUES

Whilst the community around is busy and active it is rare to see people stop and chat. Neighbours rarely drop in on one another. Sometimes neighbours are hardly more than nodding acquaintances over the fence, collecting a newspaper or reversing out of a driveway. The community has entered a period of personal territory, and individual space. While work or school communities may be strong, the sense of a local geographic community has weakened. It is hard to develop a sense of local community when people barely know who lives next door. Many people's lives now seem to revolve around their own interest groups, work situations or schools (which in a commuter suburb may be quite distant to the immediate community). How can we develop a care and concern for our neighbour when we hardly know who lives next door? The nature of community has changed from a geographic community to a community of interest, which may vary from person to person, but also diminishes the sense of belonging to a particular local place.

While a desire to cling to a homogenous core cultural identity as Australians seems to remain strong, the communal aspect of faith, at least within the Christian faith, seems to have moved in the opposite direction. While there remains a strong tendency to seek a common identity as Australians, we seem content to personalise the Christian faith, content to move away from a sense of a Christian community or common Christian identity towards a society of personalised belief. While this tendency is nothing new, tracing its roots back to the Enlightenment, is this continuing concern with the "personal" aspect of faith a mirror of the concern with the self, and the apparently increasing insecurity of identity? Charles Taylor writes "Our past is sedimented in our present, and we are doomed to misidentify ourselves as long as we can't do justice to where we come from."[8] Two questions arise. As Australians how do we identify ourselves when our dominant core culture fails to recognise both our past and the reality of our present diversity? As a Christian community within that Australian society, how do we identify ourselves as followers of Jesus when individuals

---

8. Taylor, *A Secular Age*, 29.

lay aside portions of the narrative that binds us together and defines that identity?

One of the great losses that a practical theology encounters with this personalisation of Christian faith is the loss of the transformational aspects of Christian community. This aspect of how we do theology, and how it affects the way we live our lives diminishes with the personalisation of faith. Not only does it diminish in the sense of how the individual is transformed by the Christian community, but also how the community is transformed by the Christian individual, or the Christian community within its midst. If faith is reduced to the purely personal dimension where all that is of import is the relationship between an individual and their God (whoever or whatever that God might be), then not only does the individual sacrifice the ability to be transformed by their community of faith, but the community loses the possibility of being transformed by the individual. Matters of individual conviction become merely personal choices, rather than seeds of change.

Julia Baird,[9] writing in the *Sydney Morning Herald*, reflected on an address to theological students by the Australian historian Manning Clark in the 1980s. He asked if anyone had ever seen Jesus drawn with an Australian face, and went on to reflect how the Buddha is portrayed differently throughout south-east Asia, in the image of the local people. The same might be said of depictions of Jesus and biblical events in some Latin-American and African art. The only Australian "pop-culture" imagery that springs to mind of an Australian Jesus is the artwork of Chris O'Doherty (otherwise known as Reg Mombassa), best known for his designs for surfwear.

O'Doherty has, over a number of years, created artworks around his "Australian Jesus" character. O'Doherty's Australian Jesus has reflected on a diversity of issues, including the welcome (or lack thereof) extended to refugees, the miracle of the pies and beer, gender stereotyping and other issues of the day. "Australian Jesus" is a stylistic western European pale skinned, bearded and robed Jesus, but one who has picked up a "third eye," symbol of inner knowledge or wisdom in Buddhist and Hindu thought. It is a mixture of the comfortable, with the new, of Western heritage with Eastern influence. O'Doherty's artwork engages "typical" Australians within a "typical" Australian imagery, but twists that comfortable image with contrasting cultural images and challenges. The works are cartoon-like, brightly coloured and stylised, sometimes with a slight hint of stained glass.

---

9. Baird, "Right Trumpets God and Mammon."

O'Doherty describes himself as a "nominal Christian" who likes the "idea of a lot of aspects of Jesus" but like many other Australians distrusts the "big, powerful, monolithic institution" of the church.[10] However O'Doherty's "Australian Jesus" is not simply a means of critiquing the institutional church. In fact many "Australian Jesus" images are more critical of Australian society and values than of the institutions of the church.

Many of the issues that O'Doherty has used "Australian Jesus" as a means of commenting on are issues that reflect the ambiguity of Australian identity: the mixing of traditional views of Jesus with a potent symbol of Eastern meditation and religious thought. Questioning sacred text, sacred place and symbol in the image of feeding of the 5000 at the football match with beer and pies. Questioning the role and place of women in the re-imaging of Botticelli's *Birth of Venus* with a trans-gender "Australian Jesus." Questioning Australian's concept of "fair go" and being a welcoming society in the work "Australian Jesus welcomes refugees." Each of these artworks raises questions not only for how the individual artist portrays and understands the nature of Jesus, and how that picture of Jesus comments upon the reality of Australian society, but for how the Australian community of faith responds to this individual view of Jesus. Can we see the Jesus of the church within O'Doherty's "Australian Jesus"? Is that "Australian Jesus" making a valuable critique of the ambiguities present in our Australian cultural identity?

Within the community of the church a focus on individual belief, individual salvation and the spiritualisation of our faith has led to some of our texts losing much of their force for social critique, or as means of forging a counter-cultural Christian identity. It has been too easy to accept Margaret Thatcher's notable reflection on the parable of the Good Samaritan—"No one would remember the Good Samaritan if he'd only had good intentions. He had money as well."[11] We accept a mild moralising of scripture, but overlook the radical critique Jesus makes of contemporary society. The parable of the Good Samaritan is not just a nice story told to suggest that neighbours should be kind to one another, it is a story which calls its intended hearer to "go and do likewise." It is a call not simply to be

---

10. Quotations are taken from an ABC interview with Chris/Reg by Peter Thompson, broadcast on *Talking Heads* July 23, 2007. A transcript of this broadcast is available online: http://www.abc.net.au/talkingheads/txt/s1982349.htm.

11. Margaret Thatcher, quoted in Wheen, *How Mumbo Jumbo Conquered the World.*

more caring of others, but to extend welcome, acceptance, personhood and status well beyond the accepted boundaries of the "core culture."

A similar reaction might be seen to the story of Zacchaeus. We can interpret this story in an individualist sense. Zacchaeus unquestionably is personally transformed by his encounter with Jesus. However this transformation is not a solely individual spiritual journey, restricted in its relevance to the individual concerned. It is not simply a transformation of the heart, a moment of personal conversion and salvation or even recognition of belief in the person of Jesus. The Zacchaeus story ends in the transformation of community, not just the change of heart of the individual. Not only does Zacchaeus go out and repays his charges four times over, but the community is challenged to accept this former outcast as a full and equal member. This is community restitution, rebuilding and transformation—not just a personal moment of spiritual insight.

If we can accept the radical challenge to Jesus' audience of the time, why should we reject the challenge to the "core culture" of our own time? Such stories are not simply calls to be caring and concerned members of the community, but to challenge and change our community to be the *basileia tou theou* ("kingdom" of God). In a socially and politically conservative community, such as 2079, could a re-imaging of Jesus assist in helping to affirm a new, more realistic cultural identity which recognises the presence, and contribution of indigenous and non-anglo cultures to the life of the community, and the nation?

Perhaps the flower cross is acceptable because it does not challenge either our picture of Jesus, or the self-understanding of the community. It might be a little gaudy. It is certainly noticeable and distinctive. In its own way it is comforting. But does it help a community to restructure its identity in a time of change, or does it reinforce the "core culture" of the past? Despite its lone lotus flower it remains a comfortably anglophile symbol, with flowers softening the harsh reality of crucifixion, and emphasising the colour and comfort of a European heritage.

IDENTITY, COMMUNITY, FLOWERS, AND THE FUTURE

Bechtel reminds us of the Christian quality of infiltration.[12] Metaphorical images from Jesus and Jeremiah[13] remind us that we are called by God

---

12. See Bechtel, "Salt, Yeast, Lamps, and Gadflies."

13. Ibid., which cites Jer 46:20; Matt 5:13–15; Luke 12:1, 13:21; but other readings could equally be chosen.

to infiltrate our local community. Whether it is the metaphor of salt, or light, or yeast—or indeed another, there is a consistent biblical reminder that Christians are called to act as a prophetic voice within the community. Bechtel states that "the prophets were, among other things, like the gadflies of God—landing relentlessly on the necks of the self-satisfied and arrogant, biting with a word from the Lord that refused to be ignored and refused to be shaken."[14] Much of that prophetic voice seems to have been lost. Whether this has been through being ceded to other authorities or community groups, or lost through dormancy or apathy or a combination of these and other reasons could be debated.

While we can look towards the cross of flowers, and see a symbol that in many ways is a part of the still dominant, but mercifully dying Anglo-centric core culture of 2079 and much of the rest of Australia there is another way to look towards the symbol. Imperfect and flawed as it is, it has a touch of the gadfly about it. Above all, it is there. It is a simple, visible reminder that the church continues to exist, and the message of the *basileia tou theou* continues to be proclaimed—even if somewhat more quietly and circumspectly than it could be. The challenge is to move beyond the comfort of the symbol and infuse it with an "Australian Jesus." To challenge both the Christian identity of the church, and the cultural identity of the community to see, and to move beyond, the blinkers that blind us both to the realities of the postal-code, or wider community, in which we live.

Postal-code 2079 is, like many communities within Australia, a community in flux. The identity of the community is changing, perhaps a little more slowly than some of those in Sydney and Melbourne, but changing none-the-less. There appears to be some reluctance to recognise and acknowledge this change. This may be due to a reluctance to move on from the core cultural identity of the past, or to a general apathy and unawareness of the local community in a time of individualism. Most likely it is a mixture of the two.

The church is caught in this ambiguity also. How does the local community understand its specific calling as a community of the cross in this place of changing cultural identity? How does the church stand alongside the community, but also provide a means of critiquing the challenges and the changes along the way, when its own identity is also in flux? Why continue to put up a cross of flowers? What could help this symbol speak afresh to the community that pass by, the community it stands among and over?

14. Ibid., 423.

What could so easily be read as a symbol of an outmoded church, and an increasingly inaccurate Anglo-identity could, with a little tweaking, also begin to be a signpost on the way forward. A cross of flowers reminds the community of the presence of the church. It challenges those who see it to remember that this religious community still exists. It is a reminder of God's presence among us. Now perhaps if the image can be tweaked to more visibly reflect the indigenous and cross-cultural aspects of our community, if it can reflect an openness, but not a passiveness to the community in which it is placed, then it might be a signpost towards a way ahead. It might reflect to the church community the challenge of establishing anew a sense of Christian identity, reflecting, but also critical of society and its values. It might reflect to the local community those aspects of history and current reality we choose not to see. It might reflect the ongoing presence of God. Neither Christian nor cultural identity are fixed, a genuine postalcode theology must allow the two to continually challenge and change one another. The challenge is not to find a single, genuine Australian Jesus, but to find a diversity of them, reflecting the intersection between the cross, the community culture, and the Christian narrative.

WORKS CITED

Baird, J. "Right Trumpets God and Mammon." *Sydney Morning Herald*, 16 October 2004.

Bechtel, C. M. "Salt, Yeast, Lamps, and Gadflies: Biblical Guides for Christian Identity in Civil Society." In *Christian Identity*, edited by E. van der Borght. Studies in Reformed Theology 16. Leiden: Brill, 2008.

Dixson, M. *The Imaginary Australian: Anglo-Celts and Identity, 1788 to the Present*. Sydney: UNSW Press, 1999.

Elder, C. *Being Australian: Narratives of National Identity*. Sydney: Allen & Unwin, 2007.

Hage, G. *White Nation: Fantasies of White Supremacy in a Multicultural Society*. Annandale: Pluto, 1998.

Kelly, P. "Labor and Globalisation." In *The Australian Century: Political Struggle in the Building of a Nation*, edited and introduced by R. Manne, 224–63. Melbourne: Text, 2001.

Mackay, H. *Advance Australia—Where? How We've Changed, Why We've Changed, and What Will Happen Next?* Sydney: Hachette, 2007.

Moran, A. *Australia: Nation, Belonging, and Globalization*. New York: Routledge, 2005.

Taylor, C. *A Secular Age*. Cambridge: Belknap, 2007.

Wheen, F. *How Mumbo-Jumbo Conquered the World: A Short History of Modern Delusions*. London: Harper Perennial, 2004.

5

For Christ's Sake!
Post-Coding Christ-Talk

Michael N. Jagessar

POSTAL-CODES, CONTEXTS, AND TALKING ABOUT JESUS-CHRIST: INTRODUCING THE CONVERSATION

WHEN MY FAMILY FIRST arrived in the United Kingdom, I was unaware of how postal-codes are layered and loaded markers. However, significant events occurred and opened my eyes. First, we tried to get insurance coverage for our car and the contents of our new home. Though it is one of the safest places in Birmingham to live in, the area in which we lived was considered a very high-risk area. Hence, we had astronomical prices quoted to us. The church manse was located on the borders of two postal-codes—Ladywood (B16) and Edgbaston (B17). The former is still one of the poorest wards in the whole of England whilst Edgbaston is of a quite different class. After all, it is the home of a famous cricket ground, Tolkien, lawn tennis and the University of Birmingham! Second, we started discussions around schools for our sons. The advice of my colleagues was that it would be best if our sons did not attend the local primary school, but the one slightly further on, in Harbone and in a different area and postal-code, B17.

In the event, our sons did attend the local primary school in Ladywood (B16) and the church eventually had to subsidise our very high insurance costs, as they do for most ministers involved in inner-city ministry. Postal-codes have been a strange and costly encounter for us. Living on the edge, and at the borders may be exciting, but it has a price.

I recall an advertisement of a High Street bank which carried the following line: "Never underestimate the importance of local knowledge." Local knowledge or context is always important and all sensitive theologians today affirm that theology or God-talk must be contextual—though there are still many who will operate as if *their* context is the only one that matters, or as if all who listen to or read their works ought to know their context. And if God-talk is contextual, it must also necessarily be "biographical," meaning that the people who constitute the communities that do theology must themselves, through their experiences, write or contribute to the stories. Post-coding Christology is an attempt to contextualise theology via Christology (the ways we speak of Jesus-Christ) and to do so through the views of people from a variety of locations. The concern is how our contexts and locations influence the way we perceive and speak of Jesus-Christ. In the context of Black God-Talk in Britain, my colleagues Anthony Reddie, Mukti Barton and Robert Beckford have argued for a Black Jesus who speaks for Black people. As Reddie contends: "identifying Jesus through the incarnation with Black modern day experience is essential if the Christian faith and the ongoing mission and ministry of the Church" is to reflect the reality of Black people in the twenty-first century.[1]

This paper is an attempt at a theological conversation about how Christians perceive and speak of Jesus in specific localities. Or to be more technical: it aims to map the Christ-talk, which reveals the views, of a cross-section of people located in the United Kingdom using the contexts of selected postal-codes in Britain. I need to note the provisional nature of this undertaking and that my focus is specifically on how people in congregations within one ecclesial tradition, the United Reformed Church, are talking about Jesus.

The reality is that much of our theology is located in and reflected through our christological discourse. Is there a gap between the espoused Christology of our ecclesial tradition and how the "punters" in and out of

---

1. Reddie, *Working against the Grain*, 82.

pews negotiate or re-negotiate who Jesus is for them today in their own specific contexts? What are the connections between our conversations on "the DNA" of the United Reformed Church, soteriological necessity and praxis in changing contexts, and the reconfiguring of our God-talk in the light of many variegated experiences? And does the "colouring" of our pews and ecclesial life together, through migration, make a difference to the ways we speak of Jesus-Christ? To assist me in my exploration, I will be employing liberative Black and Caribbean and postcolonial perspectives in this engagement.

WE ALL HAVE AGENDAS: MOTIVATION AND FOCUS

The motivation for this exploration has also do with my present job as secretary for Racial Justice and Multicultural Ministry in the United Reformed Church. We have declared ourselves to be a multicultural church and among my tasks is that of helping the church to practice what it means to be an inclusive community that gives agency to diverse cultural expressions of the faith. This means helping the whole church to scrutinise its theological ethos, discourse and practice of faith. And to reiterate: our understanding of and discourse about Jesus is at the heart of our vocation as a Christian community.

Hence, it is not uncommon to hear the mantra that in Christ "we are all one" and to attend gatherings where we wrestle with the question "who is Jesus Christ for us today?" These conversations tend be largely dominated by my white colleagues with a lot of lip service rendered to the "us" in the question. In practice the ethno-cultural expressions of or answers to the question are rarely given agency. And even in the "white" us—the answers tend to come from a particular class, social and gender groupings within that constituency. Moreover, among Black churches and Black congregations in the more established ecclesial traditions, there is enough evidence to suggest that the answer to the question is largely based on inherited and little interrogated christological notions with no reference to the historical and cultural implications of "us" for such Black groups. Frantz Fanon's *Black Skin, White Masks,* may be more appropriate to the way some of us answer the question. Or to be more contemporary, our Christ-talk may reflect more of a "coconut Christology"—largely white inside. However, one cannot rule out elements of signifying by the Black members.

DEFERRING TO THE PAST: TRADITION AS BOTH HINDRANCE AND OPPORTUNITY

The undertaking to reflect on "who Jesus is for us today" is not new as in faithfulness to the gospel all Christian communities in new geographical contexts have this question forced upon them. Christological reflection in the early church arose as the Christian communities attempted to discern the meaning of Jesus Christ for their lives. Any contemporary attempt to do likewise must consider the biblical record, the dogmas of the historical churches, and the living presence of Jesus Christ in the lives of Christians. In other words, any attempt at answering the "Jesus" question will necessarily have to defer to the past (while not stuck in it).

From a Reformed perspective, Brian Gerrish writes that "the Reformed habit of mind" is characterised by at least five marks: among which is *deference*—a habit of critical deference to our forbearers (not hagiography) with commitment and openness.[2] A problem is that we can get stuck "in the past" with the result that our answers to the question can also be largely hindered by past doctrines and teachings which have become solidified rather than being reflective of the dynamic ways in which, over time, Christian communities have tried to answer the question. For, as Gerrish also observes: "There will always be a sharp difference between those who understand faithfulness to tradition as the *preservation* of past doctrines and those who understand it as the recognition that past doctrines may be worthy of *development*."[3] Faithfulness to tradition has become like a chain of heavy links around ecclesial bodies.

Certainly, controlling truth under the pretext of countering heresies has been one reason why we have the Bible in its present form,[4] as well as a long proclivity towards homogenizing of the biblical stories. R. S. Sugirtharajah has rightly observed the need to expand the biblical canon and incorporate those diverse texts which were suppressed or excluded in the ecclesiastical power-game of selection and rejection.[5] He goes on to strongly contend that there is the need to move "beyond the limitations of the Jewish-Hellenistic context and pay attention also to the Jewish-Aramaic" context.[6]

2. Gerrish, "Tradition in the Modern World," 8.
3. Gerrish, *Reformed Theology for the Third Christian Millennium*, 5.
4. Boer, *Rescuing the Bible*.
5. Sugirtharajah, "Postcolonial and Biblical Interpretation: The Next Phase," 455.
6. Ibid., 456–57.

Writing from an African American perspective, Jawanza Eric Clarke observes that "Black anti-African sentiment is rooted in Black Christians'" uncritical acceptance of traditional Protestant doctrines and popular, pietistic appropriations of these doctrines, primarily the doctrine of "original sin" and the doctrine of Jesus Christ."[7] Of course, the uncritical habit is one that pervades Christ-talk in a variety of cultural contexts, leading to exclusive practices. In the World Council of Churches Document reporting on the theological consultation on "Just and Inclusive Communities" (La Paz, Bolivia, April 29–May 3, 2007) one of the challenging areas in the discussions was that of Christology. The document noted:

> It was felt that the dominant Christologies in our churches often contribute to the exclusion of the socially disempowered sections. It was felt that it is important to formulate Christologies based on concrete experiences of exclusion, emphasising the broken Jesus on the cross and the Christ who articulates and integrates the broken creation in the resurrection. This may include using language which speaks of a Jesus, the sinless and incarnated son of God, who takes upon himself the identities of those who are exploited and excluded, such as those with disabilities, of colour, of despised caste identities, of the marginalised Indigenous Peoples, abused women and children, the aged, those of different sexual orientation, etc., in order to expose the life-denying tendencies of certain cultures and structures that govern human relationships.[8]

The document goes on to argue a case for "a pluralistic understanding of Christ" that "enables the church—the body of Christ to be an inclusive community."[9]

The uncritical habit has meant, among other things, the inability to interrogate notions of "Christ" and our understanding of Jesus from our received/inherited tradition. Consequently we are unable to perceive that what passes as tradition has already been compromised. As Clark notes in the context of Christological discourse: "The bifurcation between Jesus, the human and Christ, the deity, is largely a result of the controversies within the Church that occurred centuries after the death of Jesus, based on debates about who exactly Jesus was and how the Church would officially represent him in the present and future. This orthodox construction of

---

7. Clarke, "Reconceiving the Doctrine of Jesus," 141.
8. World Council of Churches, *Just and Inclusive Communities*, 2.
9. Ibid.

Jesus Christ was performed to unify the Church and squash theological dissension and Christological controversy."[10]

Consequently, "the transformation in the Christian understanding of the 'Christ' concept stems from the influence of Greek philosophy" with the result that the notion of "Christ" was "morphed into a concept . . . that had little connection to its original meaning during the actual lifetime of Jesus. Western theology turned Christ into an exclusive deity after the death of Jesus."[11]

"Criticisms of the past," writes Talal Asad, "are morally relevant only when the past still informs the present—when contemporaries invoke the authority of founding ancestors against each other. In criticizing the dead, one is therefore questioning what they have authorized in the living."[12] When texts of the past (our tradition) still continue to hegemonically form and inform contemporary ecclesial life without being aware of the outmoded world and structures from where these have come from to form the basis for our theology and practices, it is high time for critical reflections. Here is a timely reminder from the late Edward Said: "Appeals to the past are among the commonest strategies in interpretations of the present. What animates such appeals is not only disagreement about what happened in the past and what the past was, but uncertainty about whether the past really is past, over and concluded, or whether it continues, albeit in different forms, perhaps."[13]

Most ecclesial traditions have solidified their answers to the "Jesus question" by attempting to control it, especially when the answers lean towards wayward or transgressive ways. Hence, what is most significant in the questions (who is Jesus-Christ for us today?) is the "us," a minor word with major possibilities and openings. Discourse on the "us" has been largely silent as the tendency has been to control and restrict it. This controlling has been associated with the shutting down of diverse and dissenting voices.

In deferring to the past we need to be aware of theological heritages and that these remain largely unreconstructed and at times are unhelpful framework for relevant Christ-talk. The early Christian community and their discourses are not only heavily coded; they seem to be so ingrained that we are either unable or unwilling to really expose them. For instance,

10. Clarke, "Reconceiving the Doctrine of Jesus," 148.
11. Ibid.,148–49.
12. Asad, "A Comment on Translation, Critique and Subversion," 328.
13. Said, *Culture and Imperialism*, 1.

the very early and close followers of Jesus could have imagined Jesus as God and returning in triumph without having to mention resurrection at all. A closer scrutiny on where all the emphasis on resurrection came from will point the finger to the spin-doctor "Paul."[14] Not that Paul is wrong, but that his views "was but one way of expressing early Christian faith and should not be taken as normative for all others."[15]

UN-ZIPPING CHRIST-TALK: GETTING BEHIND POST-CODING

Post-coding (zip-coding in North America) Christology is about trying to discern how the divine is spoken of and perceived to be working in specific contents. It is about the Christians' calling to faithfulness (living out of one's faith) in the particular. Hence, how Jesus is talked about in particular neighbourhoods and what difference location makes to our Christ-talk and faithfulness are both focal concerns. What is the popular view of Christ? What it is we are articulating in our Christ-talk? What sort of "take" will Black theology and post-colonial optics bring to the conversations? What, then are the implications for our theological discourse and ecclesial life? Is the controlling of "us" in our configuration of our Christology—unfaithful to the Jesus Way? Who was Jesus? What was his geographical and cultural location? Can we reclaim this Jesus, instead of the one hijacked and represented by the racist British National Party (BNP) and seen in their infamous poster campaign which cited John 15: 20, "If they have persecuted me, they will also persecute you," before asking "What would Jesus do?," and answering "Vote BNP"?[16] How does the "us" push our christological articulation to give agency to the voices and experiences of Black and Minority ethnic peoples in the UK?

The idea of using postal-codes to locate God-talk is one articulated by the Antipodean theologian Clive Pearson, borrowing from the Australian politician, Wayne Swan. Swan carried out an analysis of the economic life of Australia to reveal which postal-codes were doing better than others even though the overall economic picture may reveal another story (not dissimilar to many sociological surveys available about poverty and inclusion in the UK). In trying to uncover inequality within the nation, Swan notes

---

14. Crossan, *Jesus*, 163.
15. Ibid.,165.
16. Pigott, "Vote Jesus?" Online: http://news.bbc.co.uk/2/hi/7978981.stm.

that poverty is "often concentrated in forgotten post-codes full of people who are invisible until something goes wrong." This observation is certainly reminiscent of incidents associated with places such as Oldham, Burnley, Handsworth, and Brixton in Britain—conveniently forgotten corners, until something "explodes." Geography, demography and economy conspire to continue to cover up the inequalities and isolate some communities from the so-called prosperity of a nation in both Australia, the UK and in many of other G-20 countries.[17] Drawing on the notion of Swan, Clive Pearson develops a methodology called "doing post-code theology." According to Keith Hamilton, "post-code theology is a method of gaining clarity of what is means to be Christian in a particular context."[18] It is about contextual theology as the epistemology, that is one of "dialogue between contemporary disciples of Jesus and a particular context."[19] Given the Christological focus of most Australian churches (as it is in Britain), the methodology that Australian-based colleagues employed revolved around basic christological questions such as, *who do you say that I am? Who is Jesus-Christ for us today? Or even better, where is Jesus Christ today?* As Keith Hamilton sums up: "The work of naming our post-codes is an attempt to be contextual, an attempt to break the artificial compartmentalising of life into work, church, etc. Social analysis of the area (post-code) is thinking about who are my neighbours, what are they like, what is my neighbourhood like? One of the aims of post-code theology is to lift faith out of the church structures to interact with the neighbour. Post-code theology is public theology in which faith engages with the social situation, public issues and public consequences of Christian beliefs and convictions."[20]

Long before Hamilton and Pearson, however, theologians from the developing world have been attempting to do Christ-talk that reflects faithfulness to their contexts. They may not have done so via postal-codes, but

---

17. A significant and recent book worth considering here is Wilkinson and Pickett, *The Spirit Level: Why More Equal Societies Almost Always Do Better*. Here the authors convincingly employ statistical evidence to argue that more-equal societies enjoy better physical and mental health, lower homicide rates, fewer drug problems, fewer teenage births, higher maths and literacy scores, higher standards of child wellbeing, less bullying in schools, lower obesity rates, and fewer people in prison. Furthermore, they contend that more-equal societies also have a stronger community life and are more cohesive. The question from the perspective of this essay is what shape Christ-talk will take in more equal societies!

18. Hamilton, "Post-Code Theology," 5.

19. Ibid.

20. Ibid., 6.

the principle of context was one of their contributions about doing and practicing God-talk.[21]

While there are easier and more comfortable questions than "Who is Christ for *us* today," this one nevertheless forces us (individually and collectively) to reflect on who we are in the light of our answer to who Christ is. Besides, there is a dangerous tendency among many Christians, eager to drown themselves in the "what would Jesus do" question, as it seems to offer more ways into action and ethics. One wonders, however, whether this tendency is reflective of our deeper fear to face Jesus and answer the question. Hypothetical ethical questions may not only be "safer," they can also provide us with an opportunity to escape facing our neighbour and from being "for others" as Jesus was. Who Jesus is for us today is tied up with what we are not and maybe we are afraid to unmask for fear of the cost and implications.

A significant essay from the UK that is worth considering is that of Ann Christie entitled, "'Who Do You Say I Am?' Answers from Pews." It is based on her doctoral research. Christie explores what she calls ordinary Christology: that is the understanding of Jesus by people in the pews who may or may not have any formal theological education. To realise her purpose she interviewed forty-five "middle-of-the-road" members of the Church of England and specifically in rural North Yorkshire. She identified three main Christologies: functional, ontological and sceptical. Christie's basic concern is the gap between ecclesial (specifically Church of England) understanding of Christology and how people in pews are negotiating their beliefs in the light of their experience and existential realities. She notes,

> if adherence to christological norms is used as the criterion for what counts as Christian, then the majority of this sample of faithful churchgoers would fall outside the category of Christian. Ordinary christology suggests that what matters most in christology is not right doctrine but letting Jesus' story have its way with us. It shifts the emphasis in christology away from right belief (orthodoxy) to right practice (orthopraxis). Clearly, a disciple can follow Jesus as the Way without having to give assent to (or even

---

21. Here are some selected examples: Batumalai, "A Malaysian Neighbourology"; Bediako, "Jesus in African Culture"; Byng-Mu, "The Korean Church's Understanding of Jesus"; Costas, "Proclaiming Christ in the Two-Thirds World"; Flabella, "A Christology for Asian Women." Many more might also be cited.

understand) the christological doctrines of the Church. All the biblical models of discipleship predate any set of doctrines about him.[22]

Christie further contends that one may reasonably conclude from her sample survey that "the Christological norms which have largely governed the interpretation of Jesus for so long need to be widened (or abandoned?), and the legitimacy of a *multiplicity of christologies* recognized. Clearly not any and every interpretation of Jesus will do. There has to be some continuity between what the New Testament says about Jesus and what we say about Jesus today. But insisting upon one norm—that of Chalcedonian orthodoxy—to which all are expected to conform is at best unhelpful and at worst divisive. And besides it does not *work*."[23]

A number of insights from Christie have been helpful in locating and pushing further the responses of the participants who provided the information for this essay. These include the gaps in what ecclesial traditions teach and what people actually believe and practice; the debunking of the importance of orthodoxy or tradition as a requirement for living and walking the Jesus way; and making a claim for multiplicity in our Christ-talk. Her typologies of functional, ontological and sceptical are quite helpful in providing a framework for evaluating the responses I have received from focus groups different from that of Christie's.

CHRIST-TALK AND THE UNITED REFORMED CHURCH

In keeping with the teachings of the ecclesial traditions that make-up the United Reformed Church, one will find in its basis of union and all its theological articulation since formation (in 1972) largely traditional perspectives on Christology that are mainly formulaic in Trinitarian emphasis. Thus, in the *Basis of Union* we read, "We believe that God, in his [sic] infinite love for men [sic], gave his eternal Son, Jesus Christ our Lord, who became man, lived on earth in perfect love and obedience, died upon the cross for our sins, rose again from the dead and lives for evermore, saviour, judge and king."[24]

---

22. Christie, "'Who Do You Say I Am?' Answers from Pews," 194.

23. Ibid.

24. United Reformed Church, *Basis of Union*. Online: http://www.urc.org.uk/the-manual/62-general/the-manual/595-the-basis-of-union.html.

A revised version of the *Basis of Union*, produced in 1977, suggests an effort at connecting with contemporary British contexts, theological developments around the world, and with more inclusive language, though it is still very much reflective of the "ontological Christology" of which Christie writes, and reads thus: "We worship God revealed in Jesus Christ, the eternal Word of God made flesh; who lived our human life, died for sinners on the cross; who was raised from the dead, and proclaimed by the apostles, Son of God; who lives eternally, as saviour and sovereign, coming in judgement and mercy, to bring us to eternal life."

Over the years, in keeping with being faithful to its reforming and renewing ethos, the United Reformed Church has strived to rethink its relevance. Interestingly, we have never reflected on the Christological question, as say the French, Swiss or Waldensian Protestant Churches. Instead, we have tended to work with themes such as "Growing Up," "Catch the Vision," Vision4Life, Vision2020, and "Marketing Campaign." These themes with their usually short theological preambles that advance them, often underscore our calling with the following strap-line: "called to be God's people, transformed by the Gospel, seeking to make a difference." Interestingly, gospel is often equated with Jesus Christ, though much of the theology tends to be coming out of the mouth of Paul and the Reformers!

Our liturgies and worship services also disclose our christological views or the way we do our Christ-talk. In our services of baptism, confirmation and ordination/induction, there is a combination of historic and traditional understandings to our christological views. There is an attempt, however to also spell out what these statement will actually mean today, though not with any intentionality about the diversity of contexts. The incarnating presence and work of God in Christ and the living out of following Jesus is a strong point. Hence, the following: "Do you believe that Jesus Christ, who was born of Mary, lived our common life on earth, died upon the cross, and who was raised from the dead and reigns for evermore, is the gift of God's very self to the world? Do you believe that through him God's love, justice and mercy are revealed and forgiveness, reconciliation and eternal life are offered to all people? And will you faithfully proclaim this Gospel?"[25]

---

25. United Reformed Church, *Ministry in the United Reformed Church*.

And, "Do you accept the gift and cost of following Christ in your daily life and work? . . . With the whole Church, will you proclaim by word and action the good news of God in Christ?"[26]

It would be reasonable to suggest that the theology coming out from the "centre" tends to be more inclined towards a Trinitarian perspective, with some emphasis on the Spirit. Jesus is represented as "the ultimate expression of God's reign" but with the incarnation and resurrection given greater agency.

If we employ Ann Christie's typology to locate recent United Reformed Church christological statements and affirmations, we can discern a tendency towards a more functional typology in the sense that they are careful not to be wholly locked into traditional (ontological) typology. While we "affirm a doctrine of incarnation" as "the incarnation of God's creative, revelatory and salvific power in the person of Jesus Christ," it seems that our statements of faith do not dwell "on the incarnation of God the Son, Second person of the Trinity."[27] Perhaps, in our concern for living our faith, our confessional statements are not necessarily geared to any prolonged presentation of Jesus as God.

THE PUNTER'S TAKE: QUESTIONS, METHOD AND RESPONSES

There were four groups of people who were asked to answer one question: *Who is Jesus Christ for you/us today?* These included a group of Black, Asian, and Minority Ethnic Ministers (BAME) and laypeople (eighteen)—largely Black (Africans & Black British) and Asians (Pakistani and Koreans) with more men than women; a group of young people (31) with a good gender balance (but largely white); and two select groups (of 12) from two Synod gatherings of the United Reformed Church. The views of the members of one of the Synods were gleaned through conversations and in my following of their worship and discussion during an overnight Synod gathering. All of the participants were told about the purpose of the question and how the information would be used and all gave permission for use in this essay. While the majority of participants were from England, there are also responses from Scotland and Wales where the United Reformed Church as a denomination is also present. Also, the white group from England

26. Ibid.
27. Christie, "'Who Do You Say That I Am?,'" 187.

would have included people of Scottish and Welsh Identities, as would the responses from Scotland and Wales would have had English voices.

The groups that have responded to the fundamental question, "Who is Jesus Christ for you/us today?" reveal, among other things: a diversity of views ranging from conservative, to sceptical, to questioning, to radical, or vice versa. The responses also highlight the need for the church to reconsider ways in which it rationalises its doctrinal views with what its membership actually believes and lives by/with. If God-talk is about "the living out of faith in search of understanding and which is always rubbing shoulders with those who share the social space in which we find ourselves,"[28] then why do we still couch our doctrines in unrealistic and disconnected ways? Why is our theology often presented as if carved on granite? And, if from a Black theological perspective, God-talk for Black people in Britain is about the re-interpreting of the meaning of God as revealed in Jesus the Christ, in light of existential Black experiences in Britain—in which the Black theologian's point of departure is the existential and ontological reality of Blackness and the Black experience, in dialogue with the Bible,[29] then what is authentic about the way the Black URC members (or any Black British Christian's) answer the question, who is Jesus for us today?

FOR CHRIST'S SAKE: RESPONSES TELL LAYERED STORIES

Whatever the postal-codes, for all BAME members we are presented with the image of a Jesus of domination (king of kings; ruler, sovereign lord); one who rescues, is the answer to all problems (all I have in life), a much needed spiritual friend, protector (guardian and guide), one who leads in everything (especially difficulties), victor, healer and companion, saviour of the world, messiah who will return, great provider, one in whom God and God's reign made visible; true and faithful God who cares for all my anxieties.

Not surprisingly, a personal relationship is strong and important as will be the case for many Christians who live in and experience marginalisation. Rarely is Jesus understood as God, though the dependency on Jesus suggests an all-powerful being, who reigns to heal, rescue, and deliver. In other words, there is an underlying belief that Jesus is God. There were one or two exceptions where Jesus was represented as the only way and truth

---

28. Pearson, "The Face of Theology," 208.
29. See Jagessar and Reddie, *Black Theology in Britain*, 1.

for one respondent. One participant clearly articulated that "Jesus is the person of God expressed in human terms in all traditions and cultures." Another's response suggested a degree of sophisticated theological consideration—more like what one is "supposed" to say: "Jesus is God's gracious gift which although I did not deserve it, has brought me life eternal. Jesus invites me to join in the divine dance (*perichorisis*) of the triune unity."

We need to note here that for BAME people in the pews (as it is for many marginalised people), the significance of Jesus, while very important, is not synonymous with theological discourse and arguments about his divinity.[30] Hence, a personal and intimate relationship with Jesus, as reflected in the above responses![31] Mindful of the ways they have been enslaved, oppressed and still continue to be marginalised, BAME's Christ-talk will pay little attention to what they consider the white-magic of "turning Christ into an exclusive deity after the death of Jesus,"[32] and the dichotomising of Jesus and Christ that is linked to the strict separation of body and soul, which in the end conveniently justified the mistreatment of Black bodies.

A further observation also needs to be made: the BAME group was made up of Black and Asian British people, as well as persons from Ghana, Nigeria, Cameroon, Rwanda, Sierra Leone, India, Pakistan, South Korea, Guyana, Trinidad and Tobago, and Jamaica. While the observations made in the preceding paragraph will apply to most of the participants, it is also evident that the emphasis on the perception of Jesus differs. Hence, most Africans hold strongly the power of Jesus as healer and victor. The South-East Asians (and Africans) tend to give more agency to "saviour." And, while the responses of Black and Asian British-born respondents will reflect some of these influences, there are suggestions that they nuance their Christ-talk in different ways such as, "one in whom God and God's reign is made visible; true and faithful God who cares for all my anxieties."[33] Interestingly none of the BAME respondents made any connection between Jesus and Blackness.

One of the challenges in reading the responses of BAME people is that of the intra-diversity within and the need to discern when they are signifying. In his writings and research Anthony Reddie makes the following point to elucidate the complexity. He contends that "researchers

---

30. Brown Douglas, *The Black Christ*, 13.

31. This observation is reflected in the writings of most Black theologians, whatever their geographical location.

32. Clarke, "Reconceiving the Doctrine of Jesus," 150.

33. See Chike, *African Christianity in Britain*, 53–76.

cannot take anything Black people say verbatim as being the 'whole truth' given our propensity for signifying and the often concealed and codified nature of much that is Black religion-cultural discourse."[34] Reddie goes on to further highlight that for most Black people it was easier for Jesus to look as anyone other than themselves.[35] This may be the reason why Robert Beckford's first major piece of writing (and his best to date) has been the attempt to offer a contextualised appropriation of Jesus by locating Jesus via the Rastafarian concept of "dread."[36] According to Reddie, Beckford's project of identifying Jesus as dread relocated the historical Jesus of Palestine "alongside oppressed and marginalized people in that context, with his continued presence in Britain with equally disaffected and overlooked Black people in postcolonial Britain."[37] Whether this has made any impact on Black people's perceptions of Jesus is another matter!

If we are to employ Ann Christie's typology, most of the answers from this group will be "ontological" (mainly orthodox and inherited views). At the same time, one can discern aspects of a "functional" typology but not the way that Christie uses the term. By functional she means that which is "characterized by its lack of a doctrine of pre-existence." I would say that what is evident from the majority of the responses of the BAME members is a "pragmatic" typology determined largely by the existential experiences of Black people. In other words, what is reflected in their responses may be deeper than the usual perception of an internalised conservative kind of theology: it may be more theological realism at work here, rather than conservatism. Notwithstanding, the responses are not from the perspective of liberation, womanish, Black or Asian theologies. There is certainly no sense of critical engagement or scepticism in these answers, unless it is some form of signifying happening through these responses.

One of the Synod gatherings (London and Greater London) was predominantly white with a scattering of BAME representations. Interestingly, most of the BAME people arrived late (all dependent on public transport) and sat at the back of the gathering! Responses were received from the white respondents with images such as: saviour who leads, saviour of the world; comforter, great reformer, master, friend, fellow traveller, "the man who brought the divine and human together"; the interrogator

---

34. Reddie, *Against the Grain*, 78.
35. Ibid., 79.
36. Beckford, *Jesus Is Dread*.
37. Reddie, *Against the Grain*, 82.

(who asks why, how, and what for); the radical; the peacemaker, the lover, and the provider. Most of these respondents live in postal-code areas that will be considered rich, even though many minister and worship in quite deprived areas, which raises another set of interesting questions. The differences between responses from the predominantly BAME group and the Synod group underscore, among other things, different socialisations and a broader breadth of theological perspectives. By and large, the responses from the Synod map onto the general theological tenor of the United Reformed Church—its diversity and location in the "functional typology." One can, however, also glean from these responses, indications of Christie's third typology—"sceptical"—that is, those that will not subscribe to any orthodox view and will have a number of questions for some of the traditional views (for example, virgin birth, Jesus as God, second coming, and so on).

Significantly, the most radical and sceptical group I have interacted with is from the Synod gathering north of the English border. This was a gathering of mainly white and diverse lay and ordained members, fully aware of their complex heritages, history and struggle for Scottish identity in the context of the domination of "Brutishness." Their christological views are located in their Synod aspirations which are unapologetically theo-centric. Hence, their vision of celebrating inclusive worship and living God's unconditional love as revealed in Christ—to show that the love of God is radical in practical ways by working with all people of faiths and none for peace and justice (including the environment). In other words, God's work in and through Jesus is radically inclusive and subversive and is geared at transformation. While not explicitly stated, there is a sense of Jesus' humanity that is given more agency rather than his divinity. What is significant for me is a possible connection with the responses of the BAME group via the emphasis on Jesus' humanity. Their criticality, however, is more overt (rather than the signifying of the BAME members) in the ways they interrogate and respond to the inherited traditions around Christ-talk. In their case Christie's typology of "sceptical" (with regard orthodox views) and inclined more towards "radical" and "functional" will be more appropriate to describe their answers to the question of "Who do you say that I am?"

The group of young people, mainly from suburban contexts (with quite a few university students, some in colleges, others working) were all white, except for one person. Their responses, while reflecting their contextual realities, also highlight (even more) the thinking of young people which are largely un-orthodox and adventurous, though there are many orthodox views reflected in the responses. Their responses also suggest a great degree of their own wrestlings with the question and the ways they make sense of "Who is Jesus for us today?" Hence, the following images: guide; personal protector; "Jesus is everyone"; "weirdly-beardy" with some good ideas; best friend always present; icon and idol; a great man; everything; superman ("a normal guy with the power to save"); ideal role model of humanity (often manipulated by human beings); link between God and human beings (helping us to wrestle with ultimate questions); amazing saviour (most important person for my whole life); a role model; God's child as well as God; link to heaven, but "not the blonde blue-eyed image in churches," a storyteller, the purest form of humanity. One young person sums up the creative thinking reflected among the young people by answering the question this way: "Jesus the person—is a figure from the Bible and historical record. Jesus the Son is my friend and brother who I can always lean on. Jesus as part of the Trinity is a distant spiritual being that demands my adoration." And in good philosophical, or perhaps rabbinic, tradition, one young person had this to say, "Who is Jesus Christ—a very good question!" One even had this to say: "I wish I could have met the man," which certainly has implications about "walking in Jesus' way" and meeting Jesus today.

The responses here suggest some independent thinking, while at the same time they reflect the theological location of some of the young—that is, in the churches they come from. Interestingly, most of these young people will come from the evangelical end of congregations of the United Reformed Church, but are not necessarily averse to deploying "functional" and "sceptical" optics when it comes to answering the question "who do you say that I am?" While they may not perceive Jesus through liberation, Black or postcolonial perspectives, their understandings of Jesus will not necessarily reflect the disparity between rich and poor areas (though most would be from the richer postal-codes area and theirs was a predominantly white gathering). In fact, I would think that in this group it may just be possible for Black and postcolonial theologies to find eager listeners. No wonder churches lose their young people when they get to university as the congregation's Christ-talk and the inquiring minds of young people do not necessarily match!

QUESTIONS, CHALLENGES, AND FUTURE CONSIDERATIONS

It is reasonable to deduce that the diversity in the responses may have been influenced more by theology and experience and less by location and ethnicity/culture. In retrospect, this exercise would have benefited from another question to draw out the connection with context. The foregoing observation interests me for two reasons. Firstly, it raises the question of what is actually meant when we say that our theologising is contextual. And secondly, I had anticipated a more radical perception of Jesus from the churches located in urban and economically deprived conurbations where we also find many of the Black Majority or ethno-cultural URC congregations. I had expected that at least among some of the Black URC ministers and lay-members (mainly Ghanaian, Nigerians, Pakistani and Korean Christians) there would be some proclivity towards more liberating optics. Instead what becomes evident is a huge gulf between the responses of the younger people and that of all others. And, within each group there are also differences, suggesting that it will be risky to totalise or form a generalised/homogenous view of any of the group of those who have responded to the question. Reasons for differences within a group and between groups will vary and will include: theological background, ecclesial influence within the URC, diasporan dynamics (which will also include history and geography), and gendered, ethnic, national and cultural perspectives. Here I wish to note the timely reminder of Anthony Reddie: "researchers cannot take anything Black people say verbatim as being the 'whole truth' given our propensity for signifying and the often concealed and codified nature of much that is Black religion-cultural discourse."[38]

This notwithstanding, the critical point is the evident gap between espoused christological understandings of Jesus Christ by the United Reformed Church and how representative and significant groups in the ecclesial tradition perceive and understand Jesus. There are also differences in the ways Jesus is spoken of in terms of the economic location of peoples as seen from the particular postal-codes. Those in the richer postal-code areas do not perceive Jesus as that powerful rescuer, healer and deliverer! Clearly, some respondents say what they are "supposed" to say, giving the "appropriate" answers. Others say what they deeply believe, often traditional,

---

38. Ibid., 78.

while some are more sceptical and questioning, and some even display an adventurous spirit of creativity in employing diverse and fresh images.

Mindful of Reddie's caveat (already cited) and while it is neither easy nor wise to deduce too much from answers to this one question, I did try to locate the responses from the BAME members according to their postal-codes/areas in order to get a perspective on how their responses compare to the engagement of the URC churches in communities in those postal-code areas. The pattern suggests that many (not all) of the majority Black/Asian URC churches tend to be inward looking with little or no engagement with/in the community around them. The theology is very often conservative. It is largely the white or intentionally multicultural congregations (with Black Asian and white British ministers and elders) or Black congregations with white ministers that engage in practicing some aspect of what can be termed liberating and transforming Christ-talk. One can therefore deduce that how we think of and represent Jesus is more than likely to be reflected in our outlook on life and engagement for transformation in and beyond our immediate community. Reddie puts forward a different take on this observation, but one that enhances this observation. He writes: "Who Jesus is, is very much connected with what he does, which in turn is influenced by his appearance."[39]

Black liberation and postcolonial theology in Britain has a significant task of working with churches[40] to enable a more critical and creative engagement with the question of "who do you say that I am?" This is especially so in order to help in the process of deconstructing and interrogating inherited christological notions and giving content and language to our "ordinary" Christ-talk. How Black theological discourse can take root in pews and lives of ordinary members remains a challenge. While Black theology in Britain has done and is doing much to reclaim Jesus from Black/Asian and liberation perspectives, and while Womanish theology in particular has questioned the place of a theology of the "cross" and the need for a proper theology of the body,[41] much in the christological views

---

39. Ibid., 79.

40. Here my concern is specifically the United Reformed Church. In our journey from a multicultural to an intercultural church, the insights of Black liberation and postcolonial perspectives can contribute significantly.

41. See Pinn, *Embodiment and the New Shape of Black Theological Thought*. Pinn contends that the ideal place to begin to articulate a proper body theology is that of the body of Jesus. For the embodied nature of the Christ Event suggests that Jesus was a Jewish male with a penis. The more important question is not that he had one, but what did he

of Black theology still needs to be pushed further. This is besides the fact of the minimal engagement of Black theology with other faiths, African and African Caribbean religiosity, and the ways we continue to hold on to denominational doctrines. In terms of interrogating tradition, Black liberation and postcolonial perspectives should be mindful of the timely reminder of Musa W. Dube: "Our church traditions often name Jesus for us. But which traditions—oppressive or liberating ones? Jesus asks us, *'Who do you say that I am?'* and so it is insufficient for us to retain and use only the received Christology. Rather, we must name Christ for ourselves. Naming is often a very gendered practice."[42]

In the United Reformed Church, one of the areas to start a discussion is in terms of Jesus' Jewish identity and the implications for our own discourse on identity and how this is related to our God-talk and the shape of our liturgical life. It is timely that one of the young people rightly noted that Jesus "is not the blonde, blue-eyed image that we often see." The reality is that much of our biblical interpretation has attempted in overt and subtle ways to remove Jesus from Judaism and Jewish life. As Amy-Jill Levine notes: "If one takes the incarnation—that is, the claim that the 'Word became flesh and lived among us' (John 1:14)—seriously, then one should take seriously the time when, place where, and the people among whom this event occurred."[43]

However, in most of our congregations, the Jesus we tend to articulate actually looks like the British National Party Jesus (very Eurocentric and of a particular class), in our attempts at de-Judaising him. For as Levine also observes: "the lingering view that Jesus dismissed basic Jewish practices, such as the laws concerning Sabbath observance and ritual purity, turns Jesus away from his Jewish identity and makes him a liberal Protestant."[44]

When the BNP placed their huge billboard with Jesus on their side, British churches, especially from the historic traditions (curiously the Black Majority Churches were silent), and their theologians were running around trying to mount an opposition to what they rightly considered the pathetic hijacking of Jesus by a far-right political group. Whether Jesus needs

---

do with it. What such tough questions probe is the humanness of Jesus and how "the divine is housed in a body like ours" (97). Such an honest and challenging exploration can then open up spaces for a healthy conversation on sexuality.

42. Dube, "Who Do You Say That I Am?," 347.
43. Levine, *The Misunderstood Jew*, 347.
44. Ibid., 9.

defending is another matter! For the churches it was (and still is) clear that the policies of the BNP are highly objectionable from a gospel imperative, and their narrow and excluding nationalism especially despicable. From all of the comments from churches and pundits, however, no one commented on the white-looking Jesus that accompanied the BNP's campaign. A close-up look (of this popular image) will reveal interesting colours of Jesus' hair and eyes as imaged in the picture. Where did the BNP get their image of Jesus from? Certainly it is not their creation. British and European Christianity cannot wash its hands of this distorting image. Where did the BNP get their distorted Jesus-representation from and their obscene inclinations to link faith to British identity or nationalist tendencies? Such imaging did not drop down from Cloud Nine. And while the historic churches have spoken out against membership in the BNP and their racist policies, the reality is that Christian imaging in most churches has remained largely uninterrogated. Eurocentric indoctrination has been so thorough that Jesus, a Galilean/Palestinian Jew of the Asia Minor region, has become blond and blue-eyed. BNP's imaging of a European Jesus is the story of that unpleasant version of euro-centric Christianity "coming home to roost" and haunt Christians as we are yet to do our home-work of expunging years of bad theology and theological imaging. As noted earlier: what Jesus looks like has implications for what he means for today!

Can Black liberation theology in Britain and postcolonial optics contribute towards "saving Jesus from the church,"[45] especially among the Black Christian communities in historic ecclesial traditions? Robin Meyers asks whether churches are "toxic, beyond redemption" and should therefore be allowed to die in order to release Jesus. Meyers is all clued-up to the radical and sceptical typology when it comes to our answer to the question "who is Jesus for us today?" His observation is poignant in terms of both the challenges to the "us" in the question and the optics we employ to critically respond to the question. He writes: "We have been travelling down the creedal road to Christendom since the fourth century, when a first-century spiritual insurgency was seduced into marrying its original oppressor. Before there were bishops lounging at the table of power, there were ordinary [fisherfolks] who forsook ordinary lives to follow an itinerant sage down a path that was not obvious, sensible or safe."[46]

---

45. Meyers, *Saving Jesus from the Church*.
46. Ibid., 10.

Indeed, "we have a sacred story that has been stolen from us and in our time the thief is what passes as orthodoxy itself (right belief instead of right worship)."[47] This can be seen in the responses from the groups to the question about Jesus. While most of the respondents will not consider themselves as creedal, many by their answers suggest that they are more comfortable with "being told what to believe" than with being told how to live and what to do. The BAME participants especially seem to so personalise the relationship that the implications as a result of this relationship for engagement to transform lives is almost non-existent—at least they are not drawn out. Perhaps, this can be summed up in the words of one of the responses: "Jesus was and still is the messiah and I am waiting for him to return to earth. No postal-code will be required."

How can we move Christology from being reduced "to an arrival and a departure"?[48] How can we focus not on, are you a believer? but on, are you one who follows and walks the way of Jesus? I think that Diana Butler Bass is exactly right in observing that "people are obsessed with the second coming because deep down, they are actually disappointed in the first one."[49] Whilst identity, especially that of Jesus, is at the heart of the matter, there are also many other related doctrines that a Black liberation and postcolonial optic can help us unravel—especially the "doctrine of original sin," which is tied to our understanding of Jesus, as it actually "gives the church a permanent clientele in a salvation enterprise with no competition. You are born a hopeless sinner and sentenced to eternal damnation unless you purchase the only 'product' that can save you."[50]

Fall and redemption doctrines contribute to locking us into "belief about Jesus" rather than "invitations to follow Jesus."[51] Perhaps, this is where the BAME responses are very strong—taking the invitation to follow seriously. Yet, Minority Ethnic and marginalised peoples need to explore the connections between such inherited doctrines and the ways they are always trying to prove their worthiness. Historically, there is a connection as BAME peoples have been taught for too long to think they were never good enough. There is still need for liberation from mental slavery.

---

47. Ibid.
48. Bass, *Christianity for the Rest of Us*, 75.
49. Ibid., 220.
50. Ibid., 104.
51. Ibid., 116.

WORKS CITED

Asad, T. "A Comment on Translation, Critique and Subversion." In *Between Languages and Cultures: Translation and Cross-Cultural Texts*, edited by A. Dingwaney Needham and C. Maier, 325–31. Delhi: Oxford University Press, 1996.

Bass, D. B. *Christianity for the Rest of Us: How the Neighbourhood Church Is Transforming the Faith.* San Francisco: HarperOne, 2009.

Batumalai, S. "A Malaysian Neighbourology (To Know Malaysia Is to Love Malaysia): A Prophetic Christology for Neighbourology." *Asia Journal of Theology* 5 (1991) 346–58.

Beckford, R. *Jesus is Dread: Black Theology and Black Culture in Britain.* London: Darton, Longman & Todd, 1998.

Bediako, K. "Jesus in African Culture." In *Emerging Voices in Global Christian Theology*, edited by W. A. Dyrness, 93–121. Grand Rapids: Zondervan, 1994.

Boer, R. *Rescuing the Bible.* Blackwell Manifestos. Malden, MA: Blackwell, 2007.

Byng-Mu, A. "The Korean Church's Understanding of Jesus: An Historical Review." *International Review of Mission* 74 (1985) 81–91.

Chike, C. *African Christianity in Britain: Diaspora, Doctrines, and Dialogue.* Milton Keynes, UK: Authorhouse, 2007.

Christie, A. "'Who Do You Say I Am?' Answers from Pews." *Journal of Adult Theological Education* 4 (2007) 181–94.

Clarke, J. E. "Reconceiving the Doctrine of Jesus as Saviour in Terms of the African Understanding of an Ancestor: A Model for the Black Church." *Black Theology: An International Journal* 8 (2010) 140–59.

Costas, O. E. "Proclaiming Christ in the Two-Thirds World." *Theological Fraternity Bulletin* 3 (1982) 1–10.

Crossman, J. D. *Jesus: A Revolutionary Biography.* San Francisco: HarperSanFrancisco, 1994.

Douglas, K. B. *The Black Christ.* The Bishop Henry McNeil Turner Studies in North American Black Religion 9. Maryknoll, NY: Orbis, 1994.

Dube, M. W. "Who Do You Say That I Am?" *Feminist Theology* 15 (2007) 346–67.

Flabella, V. "A Christology for Asian Women." *Daughters of Sarah* 17 (1991) 12–15.

Gerrish, B. A., editor. *Reformed Theology for the Third Christian Millennium: The Sprunt Lectures, 2001.* Louisville: Westminster John Knox, 2003.

———. "Tradition in the Modern World: The Reformed Habit of the Mind." In *Toward the Future of Reformed Theology: Tasks, Topics, Traditions*, edited by D. Willis and M. Welker, 3–20. Grand Rapids: Erdmann, 2008.

Hamilton, K. "Postal-Code Theology: How Might God Be at Work in a Particular Place." *Out and About: Magazine of United Theological College* 19 (2009) 5–8.

Jagessar, M. N., and A. Reddie, editors. *Black Theology in Britain: A Reader.* Cross Cultural Theologies. London: Equinox, 2007.

Levine, A.-J. *The Misunderstood Jew: The Church and the Scandal of the Jewish Jesus.* San Francisco: HarperSanFrancisco, 2007.

Meyers, R. R. *Saving Jesus from the Church: How to Stop Worshipping Christ and Start Following Jesus.* New York: HarperOne, 2009.

Pearson, C. "The Face of Theology." In *Crossing Borders: Shaping Faith, Ministry and Identity in Multicultural Australia*, edited by H. Richmond and M. D. Yang, 204–17. Sydney: UCA Assembly and NSW Board of Mission, 2006.

Pigott, R. "Vote Jesus?" *Faith Diary*, April 7, 2009. Online: http://news.bbc.co.uk/2/hi/7978981.stm.
Pinn, A. *Embodiment and the New Shape of Black Theological Thought*. New York: New York University Press, 2010.
Reddie, A. *Working against the Grain: Re-imagining Black Theology in the 21st Century*. Cross Cultural Theologies. London: Equinox, 2008.
Said, E. *Culture and Imperialism*. London: Vintage, 1993.
Sugirtharajah, R. S. Postcolonialism and Biblical Interpretation: The Next Phase." In *A Postcolonial Commentary on the New Testament Writings*, edited by F. Segovia and R. S. Sugirtharajah, 455–66. The Bible and Postcolonialism 13. London: T. & T. Clark, 2007.
United Reformed Church. *Basis of Union*. Online: http://www.urc.org.uk/the-manual/62-general/the-manual/595-the-basis-of-union.html/.
———. *Ministry in the United Reformed Church*. London: United Reformed Church, 2003.
Wilkinson, R., and K. Pickett. *The Spirit Level: Why More Equal Societies Almost Always Do Better*. London: Allen Lane, 2009.
World Council of Churches. *Just and Inclusive Communities: A Report on a Theological Consultation*. April 29–May 3, 2007, La Paz, Bolivia, 1–15. Online: http://www.oikoumene.org/en/resources/documents/wcc-programmes/unity-mission-evangelism-and-spirituality/just-and-inclusive-communities/la-paz-report-just-and-inclusive-communities.html.

6

From Seclusion to Inclusion
Envisioning God's Kingdom for the Mentally Ill

Mary Pearson

WRITING IN 2005, WHILE he was shadow treasurer, Wayne Swan, published his provocative book on *Postal-Code: The Splintering of a Nation*.[1] Previously, in the portfolio of Community and Family Services, he had reflected on the task of economic management in this country. Australia was showing an increasing disparity between rich and poor, with clusters of economic and social disadvantage, areas delineated by their postal-codes. Postal-codes could be used as markers for who was winning or losing.

Swan selected the metaphor of the postal-code because these numerical labels have come to illustrate "the breakdown of the shared experience of citizenship and community."[2] Postal-codes have become more than useful categories for the sorting and delivering of mail. They have a social function which is illustrated in the not uncommon question posed at retail check-out desks where one is asked to give one's postal-code, presumably for market research. Yet postal-codes are also impersonal, numbers rather than names. They exist to facilitate electronic sorting. As tools for policy

1. Swan, *Post-Code*.
2. Ibid., 20.

makers and economic managers they obscure a more hidden story which, for the health and wellbeing of society, can take an enormous degree of courage and resolve to address.

From the perspective of Rebecca Chopp's poetics of testimony I should identify the postal-code where I work as a mental health chaplain. Concord Centre for Mental Health is a new, purpose built mental health hospital. It is situated in NSW 2139, a postal-code it shares with the neighbouring general hospital.

The mental health facility is, in many ways, deserving of its own postal-code because it is its own world: it is an environment of high fences, locked doors and security patrols, where all staff are required to wear duress alarms and police paddy wagons regularly come to drop people off. It is a place at times of heightened tension and always of human pain, alongside efforts of healing and pastoral concern. It is a world of men and women, young and old, ethnic and religious difference. Many of the people who are admitted to a mental health facility have not chosen to be there. They may have come under orders from a magistrate, a doctor or have been brought by the police and then be subject to a judicial process. They are there because they have become acutely ill, for a variety of reasons. Some admit themselves because they are no longer able to deal with the stresses of their lives. They may have become too fragile to do what would be needed to remain well or their circumstances have been too overwhelming. They are all aware of bearing a label of "mental illness" and know very well the stigma that is attached to that. Mental illness is no respecter of persons, of age, or gender and affects, in some way, 1 in 5 people across the whole of society.[3] Some feel shame at being in a psychiatric hospital and do not want friends or family to know where they are. Their individual experiences of illness are emphasized by now being in a place where they are surrounded by others who may be even more unwell, seemingly uncontrolled, agitated or deeply depressed. Their own struggle to hold onto their identity is now compounded by that of those around them. They are locked in, only able to go out with permission as they are deemed well enough. They may, or may not, understand that these conditions are there for their own good. Mental illness can become

---

3. Wesley Mission Research Department, *Living with Mental Illness: Attitudes, Experiences and Challenges*, found the incidence to be between 22 percent (diagnosed mental illness) and 36 percent (including diagnosed and suspected mental illness). The Australian Bureau of statistics figure of 20 percent reflects experience of mental illness over a twelve-month period. The Wesley Mission's research makes sense in the lifetime prevalence of mental disorders.

the over-riding theme. They are in a place, a hospital, which has its own postal-code, a number that would seem to denote a struggle for identity and well-being in the face of acute and pointless suffering.

Most of those who are resident look towards leaving this postal-code: to being well enough to return to family and friends; to their own space, work, study and familiar routines. Some leave with anxiety about how they will cope. For some, their illness has led to homelessness and they worry about where they will find housing in which they can feel safe; where they will find support and people who will understand and care. A support worker for Wesley Mission's Homeless Service expresses the fragility of the situation where "there's nowhere for them to go, no one will take them. They don't fit into whatever box has been set up in the other services."[4] Whether they appreciate it at the time or not, this postal-code furnishes a degree of safety, protection, and time to reassess.

As a chaplain one has to learn to hear behind the illness, the psychoses and delusions; to identify the pain and loneliness, the grief and fear that are normal human emotions. Sometimes people are too unwell to engage for very long at all or to feel able to imagine the future. Sometimes it is a long journey towards a level of wellness: patients may be in hospital for weeks or even months. For those who work to care for patients, the stories that people carry in their lives raise the difficult questions that, for Christians, bear the challenge of theodicy. Why do some people, who have had an ordinary childhood and adolescence, become ill at a time when their lives would otherwise have begun to flower? What hope can they now find? Where is the meaning to be discovered in the lives of those who will always have to contend with hearing voices that constantly disturb? What kind of society have we become that so many young people's lives are ruined by drug-induced psychoses and scarring addictions? Why is there this difference? What can we do?

In Australia's multi-cultural, multi-faith society, we are very aware of difference and of the need to strengthen the civil society. Even before the events of September 11th, 2001, polarized the world into Christian/Western and Muslim/Middle Eastern other, there was discussion about the breakdown of the social fabric of society. The origins of this very practical debate lay in the opening up of immigration policy and the introduction of politics of multiculturalism. The growing discrepancy between the well off and those who were disadvantaged in an era of a competitive free market

---

4. The Wesley Report July 2007, *Living with Mental Illness*, 78.

led Eva Cox to deliver her 1995 Boyer Lectures on "A Truly Civil Society." One of the key dimensions for a healthy society, she argued, of was what she calls the "thin," casual, and non-intimate relationships that permeate society. Much of our feeling of wellbeing comes from the way we perceive the world around us and whether or not it can carry our trust. Cox concluded that "we make sense of the world around us, of our daily life and our usual and unusual experiences, by using our interpretations of experiences, direct and indirect, to frame our expectations. If we expect pleasant or unpleasant incidents, we act accordingly. We frame scripts in which we articulate our expectations of how we will interact with others which will fit within the way we see the broader narratives of the world around us."[5]

Our attitudes to those around us, to those who are different, shape the way in which our society functions. Suspicion of the stranger, the alien, of those who are different is not new, although it has been fed by the often divisive rhetoric of politics in the post-9/11 world. The first known map of the world, the Mappa Mundi, was drawn in 1493 by Hartman Schedel. The large mass of the unexplored southern hemisphere is inscribed with the words, "Here be Monsters." The way in which we question those attitudes and unconscious responses to the unfamiliar or potentially threatening is crucial to the growth of our communities. How do we deal with our fear of the "other"?

The Christian tradition demonstrates a tension in response to such fear. The practice of hospitality, which is deeply rooted in Hebrew culture, stems from the commandment "You shall love your neighbour as yourself" (Leviticus 19:18). Christine Pohl describes hospitality as being the pillar on which all morality rested. Not only were the people to avoid mistreating the stranger, they were "actively to seek their wellbeing."[6] For Christians, this was demonstrated in Jesus' life and teaching. The parable of the Good Samaritan (Luke 10: 25–37) is often cited as an example. Against this, the fear of the "other" has also led to attitudes which are seen most obviously in respect to those of other faiths. These were categorized by Alan Race as "exclusivist," "inclusivist," or "pluralist."[7] They are more subtly experienced by those with disabilities.[8]

---

5. Cox, "Faith in the Public Forum?," 74.
6. Pohl, *Making Room*, 29.
7. Race, *Christians and Religious Pluralism*.
8. Eisland, *The Disabled God*.

The term "other" can become a category that embraces any who are different in terms of culture, gender, sexuality, faith, economic status. It implies a boundary around narrowly prescribed relationships of similarity. Much has been written in recent years, exploring such difference. Miroslav Volf writes out of his personal experience of the effects of civil war in the Balkans in his highly regarded *Exclusion and Embrace*. In examining responses to ethnic difference that are still so evident today, he cites Charles Taylor: "No recognition or misrecognition can inflict harm, can be a form of oppression, imprisoning someone in a false, distorted and reduced mode of being."[9]

Volf recognizes that there are a number of ways of approaching the issues of identity and otherness but suggests that they all share a common concentration on the social arrangements that are needed to accommodate difference. He makes clear that these arrangements are not the field of theology. It is not the organization of society as such that interests him. Rather, reflecting Cox's stance, Volf's overriding concern is with how we are social agents, exploring "what kind of selves we need to be in order to live in harmony with others." Being a theologian himself, Volf sees a great need in current society for further theological reflection on what it means to be a social agent and not simply be confined to stock disciplinary questions of what it means to be human and a disciple of Christ. It is an issue of moral responsibility. For a healthy, social society, the role of the individual and the relationships between individuals is of great importance, yet the trend appears to be away from such responsibility. Zygmunt Bauman has argued that modernity is "prominent for the tendency to shift moral responsibilities away from the moral self either towards socially constructed and managed supra-individual agencies, or through floating responsibility inside a bureaucratic 'rule of nobody.'"[10]

The pluralist nature of a liberal secular democracy in an age of enhanced global intersection encourages the recognition of difference. For Swan, Cox, Vole and Bauman that difference is cultural, social and ethnic. Their list is not exhaustive. My intention is to focus on an area where "otherness" comes close to home and is most often regarded with fear and suspicion—that is, the difference of mental illness. Here the fear of the other can lie within the self and spill over into a community response.

---

9. Charles Taylor, *A Secular Age*, 25, quoted in Vole, *Exclusion and Embrace*, 19.

10. Bauman, *Life in Fragments*, 99.

Fear is a complex emotion. It is a necessary response to danger, provoking the "flight or fight" reaction. It is universal but may also develop out of proportion to the actual danger and become a phobic anxiety.[11] Fear of the other can lie within the self, engendered by experience. The mother of a young man with drug induced paranoia and bi-polar disorder says "You live with fear. I could get a phone call any day to say that Richard has killed himself or been beaten to death."[12] Such fear arises out of love and compassion for the sufferer. Fear in relation to mental illness has many aspects. For some people it still carries echoes of a taint on the soul and age-old connections with demon possession. As a mental health chaplain I have been asked, "What do you think about demons?" It was not an academic question. It was asking if I believed that an individual had been taken over by a malevolent power or powers. It is the question that can open up a visceral debate, breaking through protective barriers and challenging comfortable beliefs. Perhaps, unconsciously, it approaches the heart of the deep seated fear of mental illness.

It is important to examine this fear and what underlies it. In his book *Common Humanity*, Raimond Gaita, who understood from first hand experience the trauma of mental illness, emphasizes the important connection between faith and struggle. If we are to reflect on the nature of fear, of moral responsibility, theology and the place of religion in society, what Gaita says has a particular relevance. "It seems essential to the very idea of a religion that its adherents must claim it deepens our understanding of what matters to us, especially to those big facts that define the human condition—our vulnerability to suffering, our mortality, our sexuality."[13] One could add "our mental frailty."

How then do we respond when religion deepens fear rather than understanding? Talk of demons is not part of mainstream theological debate. If we are to face the fear of mental illness that is present in society and be able, as communities and individuals to reach out to the sufferers, we need to examine the way in which we think of demons, of talk of the devil. Walter Wink opened up this issue and its underlying development from the scant mention of Satan in the Hebrew Scriptures, on through the presence of Satan as clarifying faith for Jesus in the gospels until in the early church Satan became evil personified and separate from God. In this way

11. Hicks, *Fifty Signs of Mental Illness*, 121.
12. The Wesley Report 2007, *Living with Mental Illness*, 81.
13. Gaita, *Common Humanity*, 239.

Wink demonstrates how culture and circumstance affected understanding. Satan was changed from acting as God's servant to acting as the Evil One. However, Wink cautions about seeing this as having become a choice based on personal theological preference and cites passages by the same gospel authors in which Satan acts as both (see especially Luke 4:1–13). For Wink, it is of prime importance to listen for "every word that proceeds from the mouth of God," otherwise we polarize and personify Satan as the evil one, which breeds a paranoid view of reality and justifies the demonizing of opponents. "It prevents us loving our enemies. It legitimizes violence against those whom we regard as evil." Not only on a personal level but as societies there is a danger that a personified evil "induces blindness to the radicalism of evil, trivializes the struggle for conscious choice, and drives the satanic underground, converting the unconscious into a cesspool of erupting nightmares." "Perhaps," Wink concludes, "in the final analysis Satan is not even a 'personality' at all, but rather a function in the divine process."[14]

The gospels give us many examples of Jesus casting out demons. While Wink would challenge the thinking that too easily finds answers in talk of Satan and demons, we are still left with the reality of mental illness that has always been part of human history and how we may approach those for whom there is no prospect of cure but only of management. A fundamental question is always present: what does healing mean in the context of mental illness? It hovers over life within the psychiatric hospital.

Reflecting on Jesus' healing ministry, Donald Capps' book, titled *Jesus the Village Psychiatrist*,[15] emphasizes the social aspects of illness and the somatic nature of much suffering. He argues that Jesus was able to see this and to deal with the more hidden nature of people's afflictions. It was in this way that healing took place for an individual and of the context in which they belonged. This is an important connection, even though in the psychiatric hospital there are clearly those whose brain dysfunction can only be controlled by medication, prescribed by a psychiatrist with in-depth knowledge of mental illness. There are many examples of patients who have been discharged feeling well and have then stopped taking medication, only to need hospitalization again as a result. Nevertheless, as Capps might

---

14. Wink, *Unmasking the Powers*, 32.

15. Capps, *Jesus the Village Psychiatrist*. It is interesting that he should use the term "psychiatrist" rather than "psychologist," because he infers a mental illness, yet talks primarily of those with more generalized physical ailments. The one instance of "demon possession" he looks at is the story of the boy who had a seizure (Mark 9:14–19), which he is able to regard as a form of epilepsy.

suggest, there are also always those whose situations are compounded by societal or familial dysfunction whose well-being would be greatly aided by being supported within a society that could accept a role of responsibility and care and have the courage to see itself as part of the story of wellbeing. Anyone who suffers from mental illness struggles with wearing a label of difference imposed by the community that is often wary of becoming involved. The moral responsibility is there to act as social agents. "Healing" can only happen within this context.

Within the postal-code of the psychiatric hospital, questions about the role of the institution and the moral responsibility of the whole of society have particular focus. The work of healing and wholeness does not finish when a patient is discharged. We know that the stigma of mental illness is deeply felt, so it is necessary to look further at the things that affect the response of our communities and society. Michel Foucault has argued in his *Madness and Civilization* that madness is not a natural or unchanging thing; it depends on the society within which it exists.[16] Various cultural, intellectual and economic structures determine how madness is known and experienced within a given society. In Renaissance times the experience of madness was integrated into the rest of the world, but by the nineteenth century it had become known as a moral or mental disease. Foucault saw madness as being located within a certain space in society, a space whose shape, and its effects on the sufferer, depend on the society itself. That space has changed over time. In the last century it has moved on from the asylum to the psychiatric hospital and from there to increasing but fragile links into the community.

This latter movement has changed things for people who were once forced to live always separated off, and, in some ways protected, in the asylums of hospitals. Now, on reaching a level of wellbeing, they have to cope within local communities. Here they are confronted by the difference that their illness makes. In the very diverse communities of our cities, this is a particular separation. Reports from the Mental Health Council of Australia note how, following a commitment in 1992 by Health Ministers to redress decades of neglect, policies changed. One of the key reforms was the desire to support sufferers in the community. This policy was reviewed by the Mental Health Council in 2002. It found that "despite the efforts of committed politicians, government officials, service providers and community advocates, we do not have an effective or accessible mental health system

16. Foucault, *Madness and Civilization*.

... People with mental disorders, and their families, feel frustrated and let down by the system ... It is recognized that mental health reform is difficult—requiring years rather than months to occur—but the current inadequate pace of reform condemns the disadvantaged and ill members of our community to more years of abuse, neglect and poor mental and physical health."[17]

Such findings do more than highlight a failure of policy. They also point to the sidelining of mental illness in society. A report by The Wesley Mission, entitled *Living with Mental Illness*, found that while there is increasing understanding and acceptance of people who suffer from depression, there is less acceptance of those with schizophrenia or bi-polar disorder. The level of comfort in the community also depends on how close was the knowledge of the sufferer and on factors such as whether the person was in a position of responsibility within the workplace.[18] Writing in the *Medical Journal of Australia*, Barbara Hocking notes that "many people with schizophrenia say that the stigma and prejudice associated with their illness is as distressing as the symptoms themselves."[19] Stigma contributes to loneliness, distress and discrimination against people with a mental illness and their families. This stigma is not just felt in attitudes but in practical ways such as discrimination in housing, education and employment. The result is that many people are reluctant to seek help and cooperate with treatment. Lack of self esteem not infrequently leads to suicide.

While Cox and Volf have indicated the pervasive undercurrent of fear of ethnic, social and economic difference, the space of mental illness within society of which Foucault speaks is not delineated by these more commonly held barriers but denotes an environment of pain. A worker from the Wesley Counselling services commented: "People with mental illness feel like they don't fit. Even if they wanted to go somewhere, they don't fit easily there."[20]

What, then, might this mean for society and the practical issues that are raised for those whose continuing wellbeing requires understanding? It is apparent that the dynamic between fear of difference and moral responsibility has a particular shape with mental illness. There have been conflicting

17. Online: http://www.mhca.org.au/AboutMentalHealth/factsheets/mentalhealth reform.html.
18. The Wesley Report July 2007, *Living with Mental Illness*, 43–45.
19. Hocking, "Reducing Mental Illness Stigma Discrimination."
20. The Wesley Report, July 2007, *Living with Mental Illness*, 54.

societal pressures in regard to the treatment and accommodation of those who suffer from such illnesses.[21]

Against this evident theodicy the Christian faith turns to the person of Christ. Indeed it can find in Jesus someone who was himself stigmatized as being mad or as acting for Beelzebul (Matt 12:24). The cross itself is a symbol not just of suffering but of God's involvement in the pain of the human condition. It is also a symbol of the struggle against injustice and oppression. Jürgen Moltmann is one who has written about the theology of the cross, linking back to Luther's *theologian cruces*. For Molt Mann, the cross is the "key signature" of life.[22] Douglas John Hall writes about the theology of the cross[23] in order to counteract christologies of glory and success that can cocoon us in our comfort zones—in this case our postal-codes. In different ways, the cross has significance for those who suffer from mental illness. The apparent pointlessness of what happened to Jesus that first Easter impacts on Christians each Good Friday and is an experience very real to those who suffer from a psychiatric disorder.

In the psychiatric hospital, and especially amongst those who are most acutely unwell, the cross is often seen as something that offers protection from the voices, paranoia or darkness that threatens them. It speaks to them of a recognition of their individual battles and of the care that they so need. At the same time, the Good Friday message of God's identification in Christ with deep human pain, unjustly suffered, is deeply felt.

Theodicy in any circumstance is confronting. In this very particular suffering of mental illness, we face the tension of suffering that both demands our compassion and understanding and also the fear that tends to exclude. Julia Kristeva, who writes about "foreignness," expresses attitudes that could equally apply to those who are set apart by mental illness. She writes of (an invitation) "to discover our disturbing otherness, for that indeed is what bursts in to confront that 'demon,' that threat, that apprehension generated by the projective apparition of the other at the heart of what we persist in maintaining as a proper, solid us."[24]

---

21. The Wesley Report notes the reluctance within society to trust people with mental illness, especially schizophrenia. Only 34 percent of people surveyed said that they would be comfortable with their child sharing a flat with someone with a mental illness.

22. Moltmann, *The Crucified God*, 72.

23. Hall, *The Cross in Our Context*.

24. Kristeva, *Strangers to Ourselves*, 192.

To do this, to face our own inner demons, asks us to look suffering in the face and accept its reality, its necessity and its inescapability. It raises profound christological questions about the way in which we accept the necessity of taking up the cross and not, like Peter, rejecting it. It involves accepting the consequences of a shared humanity. It is counter-cultural as it asks us to widen the tent rather than retreating into the safety of the familiar and the chosen, or shutting the gates on anyone who might disturb our peace.

This is part of creating a healthy society. Zygmunt Bauman writes about the desire to ensure that our environment is healthy. Yet, as he says, "You tend to seek a remedy for the discomforts of insecurity in a care for safety, that is for the integrity of your body with all its extensions and front-line trenches—your home, your possessions, your neighbourhood. As you do so, you grow suspicious of the others around you, and particularly of the strangers among them, those carriers and embodiments of the unpredicted and unpredictable."[25]

It is not just for the care of those with a psychiatric problem that we need to confront our fear of mental illness, but for our own health and that of our society.

Postal-codes may be a useful tool for social analysis. They may denote areas of economic and cultural difference. It is also true that, wherever we may live, the "thin" relationships that Cox mentioned are often stretched to breaking point with the stresses of our fast paced, economically pressured life. It is an environment where stress and depression are increasing. These are no longer taboo subjects. We have been forced to face them. Society is less accepting of those who suffer from schizophrenia or bi-polar disorder, yet they affect people from ever strata of society. They do not cluster around particular postal-codes. Mental illness raises important theological and pastoral, economic and strategic questions. It asks us not only about the way in which we acknowledge the suffering and fear that may lie not far below the surface, but also whether these things are allowed to affect the response that is made at a personal, community and political level. While postal-codes may be used as a labelling or categorizing device, mental illness asks us to see beyond the labels that stigmatize and decide whether we can deal with both the seclusion and inclusion that the sufferers may need. It asks us how we envisage the kingdom of God.

---

25. Bauman, *Community*, 145.

WORKS CITED

Bauman, Z. *Community: Seeking Safety in an Insecure World.* Themes for the 21st Century. Cambridge: Polity, 2001.

———. *Life in Fragments: Essays in Postmodern Morality.* Oxford: Blackwell, 1995.

Capps, D. *Jesus the Village Psychiatrist.* Louisville: Westminster John Knox, 2008.

Cox, E. "Faith in the Public Forum?" In *Faith in the Public Forum*, edited by N. Brown and R. Gascoigne, 63–77. ATF Series 1. Adelaide: Australian Theological Forum, 1999.

Eisland, N. L. *The Disabled God: Towards a Liberatory Theology of Disability.* Nashville: Abingdon, 1994.

Foucault, M. *Madness and Civilization: A History of Insanity in the Age of Reason.* Translated by R. Howard. New York: Random House, 1965.

Gaita, R. *Common Humanity: Thinking about Love & Truth & Justice.* Melbourne: Text, 1999.

Hall, D. J. *The Cross in Our Context: Jesus and the Suffering World.* Minneapolis: Fortress, 2003.

Hicks, J. W. *Fifty Signs of Mental Illness: A Guide to Understanding Mental Health.* New Haven: Yale University Press, 2005.

Hocking, B. "Reducing Mental Illness Stigma Discrimination—Everybody's Business." Online: https://www.mja.com.au/journal/2003/178/9/reducing-mental-illness-stigma-and-discrimination-everybodys-business/.

Kristeva, J. *Strangers to Ourselves.* Translated by L. Roudiez. European Perspectives. New York: Columbia University Press, 1991.

Moltmann, J. *The Crucified God: The Cross as the Foundation and Criticism of Christian Theology.* Translated by R. A. Wilson and J. Bowden. London: SCM, 1974.

Pohl, C. H. *Making Room: Recovering Hospitality as a Christian Tradition.* Grand Rapids: Eerdmans, 1999.

Swan, W. *Post-Code: The Splintering of a Nation.* North Melbourne: Pluto, 2005.

Volf, M. *Exclusion and Embrace: A Theological Exploration of Identity, Otherness, and Reconciliation.* Nashville: Abingdon, 1996.

Wesley Mission Research Department. *Living with Mental Illness: Attitudes, Experiences and Challenges.* Wesley Report, July 2007. Sydney: Wesley Mission, 2007.

Wink, W. *Unmasking the Powers: The Invisible Forces That Determine Human Existence.* The Powers 2. Philadelphia: Fortress, 1986.

7

Wandering

Stephen Burns

> My mind has been wandering,
> I hardly noticed...[1]

IN THIS ESSAY MY mind wanders across several ways in which a locality might be mapped, in more and less detailed and technical ways, but all of which offer questions, depth, caveats, and complements to a postal-code theology. I begin and end with reflection on worship.

STARTING WITH STATIONS

On July 18, 2008, during the program of World Youth Day events, the streets of the central business district of Sydney became scenes for a representation of the Stations of the Cross, "a travelling dramatised re-enactment of the last days of Jesus' life."[2] In a contemporary gesture, images of this version of the longstanding devotional practice of the Stations were projected on to a screen at the crypt of St. Mary's Cathedral, the city's mock-gothic

---

1. Sylvian, "A Fire in the Forest."
2. http://www.zimbio.com/pictures/ogSq-OAjqgz/Stations+Cross+Enacted+Across +Sydney+World/ 35hxsECkFPh.

Roman Catholic mother church. In the streets and on the screen, thousands of people followed the re-enactment of Jesus' last journey.

Maybe the Stations can be thought of as a kind of proto-public theology? The origins of the Stations are in fourth century practice in Jerusalem, sometime later transported to Rome, where, it seems, the liturgies of Lent were marked around different districts of the city. Where depended on how the liturgy might be imagined in relation to particular places. The main assembly of the day might be located at a church dedicated to a saint who featured prominently in the gospel reading of the lectionary sequence of the day. So if, say, Mary featured in the reading, the liturgy might be centred on a building dedicated to her. A procession would lead to that church from the one where the previous day's liturgy was celebrated and would lead on to the place where the next day's service would take place. Not only was the liturgy offered both inside and outside of the churches' buildings—so that we can trace one immediate connection with the meaning of liturgy as "public service"—but it was also contextualized in the sense of attempting to draw the residents of a particular neighbourhood into the liturgical action by identifying with one of their local landmarks.

This memory of ancient practice, brought vividly alive during World Youth Day, is also an interesting (sort-of) precedent for thinking about "postal-code theology." But clearly the correspondence is not exact. Yet the very point that correspondence is imperfect can itself serve as a reminder of the importance of wider views of context when thinking about a particular district with a postal-code. As an example of the ways in which thinking shifts with contexts, postal-codes in my native England are quite different to postal-codes in the country where I am now resident, Australia. In Sydney, where I live, postal-codes refer to districts of the city, sometimes each covering densely populated areas embracing perhaps thousands of inhabitants. In England, postal-codes very oftentimes refer to much more specific localities. So it is not uncommon for (odd-numbered) houses on one side of the street to have one postal-code, whilst others (even-numbered) have another. A postal-code may be shared by only two or three other buildings—or, in some rare cases, none. In the nearby Republic of Ireland, nowhere in the whole country has postal-codes; addresses lack them altogether. People live without them.

JUXTAPOSING DIFFERENT MAPPINGS

Juxtaposing different "mappings" begins to yield a descriptive richness about particular postal-codes. These further mappings are able to nuance attention to localities in more particular ways than even "small" postal-codes. At least some of these dynamics can be seen at work across the postal-code in which I grew up, CA28 6TH. In the first place, the postal-code itself: CA28 identifies the town in which I lived—Whitehaven, on the western coast of Cumbria. The second cluster of numbers and letters, 6TH, identifies a very particular district of the town. Less than ten houses share this postal-code, all close to a minor road junction—to be precise, where The Crest and Ruskin Drive meet Highfields—on the Hillcrest housing estate. 6TH identifies houses on one side of Highfields at this particular junction. Even-numbered houses further down the road have another postal-code, and odd-numbered houses across the road have another postal-code again. It takes a minute or two to walk through this postal-code, and merely seconds to drive through it.

One of the other layers to overlay on a postal-code is found in the observation that both sides of my road were in Hillcrest political ward. This was one of the ten most so-called "privileged" wards in the north of England, with a concentration—across several postal-codes—of well-paid skilled and semi-skilled workers then employed at the nearby and controversial nuclear power-plant, Sellafield. (The novelist Barbara Kingsolver, better known for her *Poisonwood Bible*, has a book about it, called *Sellafield*, which is banned in Britain). However, the town—identified by postal-code as CA28—also enveloped one of the most "deprived" wards in the north of England, Mirehouse West. The postal-code descriptor CA28 therefore harboured a wide spectrum of experience, economic and otherwise, that might only be surfaced by more particular kinds of awareness than the broad postal-code points towards.

"DEPRIVATION" AND "REGENERATION"

In England, political wards are the primary subject of the so-called Indices of Deprivation, most recently compiled in 2007 by what in 2000—the year on which I shall focus here—was the government department of the Environment, Transport and the Regions (later disbanded and re-branded in terms of "community"). This wide study was developed by researchers at the University of Oxford and charted the interplay of six "domains"—1. income (with a subset on child poverty); 2. employment; 3. health deprivation and disability; 4. education, skills and training; 5. housing; and 6. geographical access to services—ranking the 8414 political wards in England from most deprived (1) to most privileged (8414). One particular sub-domain was also singled out, so although also located as a strand of the income domain, a separate child poverty index was collated which identified the extent of persons under sixteen years of age living in low income households in each ward. To produce the final score, or "index of multiple deprivation," each of the six domains was weighted, though not equally, so income was weighted at 25 percent of the overall score; employment at 25 percent; health deprivation and disability at 15 percent; education, skills and training at 15 percent; housing at 10 percent; and geographical access to services at 10 percent. In my home town, all CA28, among the several political wards, Hillcrest is ranked at 6365, and Mirehouse West at 84.

At the time of the indices' publication in the year 2000, I no longer lived in Whitehaven, but in Gateshead, on the south banks of the Tyne with central Newcastle to the north, in north-east England. I worked as director of an "urban mission centre," a joint venture between the University and Diocese of Durham, based in a so-called "urban priority area" as the Church of England's influential 1985 report *Faith in the City: A Call for Action by Church and Nation*[3] named clusters of concentrated urban poverty. At the time, in the fourteen or so mile trip from the theological college in Durham to Gateshead parish, students would travel through around 90% of the scale of the Indices of Deprivation. The college itself was located on the Durham Peninsula—the land around that city's majestic Norman cathedral—in the ward of Nevilles Cross, in the top ten percent. The parish of Gateshead, which rather roughly mapped onto Bede ward, was in the bottom ten percent. Much of the journey between the two can be made on the major trunk road, the A1; but travel on public transport—by bus, especially—allowed some of the differences of place in the scale to be *seen* as the bus traipsed through a hotch-potch of diverse inter-connected built environments. The parish itself was, unenviably, the poorest parish in the poorest diocese in the country, which is not to say that it was the poorest parish in the country, but to indicate something more general about its "position"—as well as about the way that statistics, and the realities they may reveal or disguise, can be

---

3. Now available online: http://www.cofe.anglican.org/info/socialpublic/urbanaffairs/faithinthecity/fitc.html.

variously presented. Nevilles Cross was ranked 8261 of the 8414 wards in England, Bede 117. Bede's ranking was much higher than it would have been if "access to services" had not been a domain in the indices, for whilst in each of the categories the ward languished low in the rankings (106 for health and disability, 121 for employment, for example), in this aspect it soared (6770)—access to services was relatively abundant, because quality (not to say length) of life as measured by the other registers was weaker, and "professional" resources had been introduced to attend to—other people's, "non-professionals"—"problems." Very significant financial investment in services had not, however, dramatically raised the rankings for other domains. So the indices raise questions about by what means and in whose company it is possible to "raise" the situation of deprived persons. And just as the "poverty" of a parish can be presented in different ways, the very organization of the indices itself also invites questions about the "politics" of its categories, and the extent that their identification and presentation may be politically convenient, "massaged," hidden, and in other ways "fixed": the exercise is skirted by questions of "how to distinguish real change over time from that caused by small modifications in data or methodology."[4]

By the time the Indices of Deprivation was updated in 2004, significant criticism of it has been registered and amendments to its methods which allowed for smaller pockets of deprivation or privilege to be recognized within the wider categories of wards. Hence, it became possible to identify with greater specificity than the previous more general surveys the interplay of the domains in the local terrain. This revealed more textured ways in which relative wealth, health problems, educational opportunity, and so on, are distributed. This more textured perspective of the 2004 exercise was perhaps especially important in urban settings, as poverty and wealth are so oftentimes cheek by jowl in urban environments: "mosaics of geographically inward-looking communities,"[5] spatially proximate but disengaged from each other, with little if any of the creative intermingling, or cultural mixture that are sometimes lauded as key to urban potential. In cities especially, broader categories can mask social realities that only become apparent when looking at a smaller framework. Of course, I speak here about the analysis of statistics, for the shifts if not disjunctions in urban environments can sometimes be quite readily evident by travelling

---

4. Department for Communities and Local Government, *Updating the English Indices of Deprivation 2004*, 8.

5. Amin et al. *Cities for the Many Not for the Few*, 41.

through particular neighborhoods—perhaps especially so when travelling *on foot*. Roads that sever districts from one another (with little or no safe provision for pedestrians to cross roads), high walls—perhaps topped with razor-wire or broken glass—and so-called "gated communities" are just some of the seems between pockets within wards which are visible to the onlooking eye, and sometimes very difficult for bodies to traverse.

To speak of walking and looking is also to recall that "deprivation" *always* has an "anatomy." When David Pacione writes of the "anatomy of multiple deprivation" he refers to a circle of low pay, dereliction, delinquency, unemployment, poor services, one-parent families, poor housing, ill-health, powerlessness, stigmatisation, vandalism, poor schooling and homeless, all of which are held together by the central problems of poverty and crime.[6] Low pay is connected to dereliction, delinquency to unemployment, and so on, as sinews in the body. John Vincent extends the metaphor to put "faces" onto this "anatomy," insisting from a Christian perspective that the issues of deprivation are best discussed and addressed with a focus on: low-paid *people*, derelict *human* environment, delinquent *children*, segregated *persons*, and so on.[7] Such a humanizing perspective may be a distinctively religious or theological approach to the issues that need to be faced, and in some if not all postal-codes insistence on this humanizing will be an invaluable piece of ministry.

Also of relevance here is a critique that rumbled under New Labour's initial attempts to revivify impoverished urban environments with so-called "regeneration" projects, part of New Labour's rhetoric that within ten years of their administration no one in Britain would be prejudiced against because of where they lived. In fact, in Gateshead, this rhetoric coincided with some creative entrepreneurship by the local council, also Labour. They fixed the very practical problem of a collapsing disused mineshaft running under the A1 by filling the mine with concrete as a base for the largest piece of public sculpture in Europe, the Angel of the North, paid for largely by arts grants to support this new addition to the local landscape. Following were new initiatives to renew riverside wastelands: a derelict mill transformed into what would become the UK's second largest contemporary art space (after Tate Modern), the Baltic; the Sage, an "opera house" (loosely modelled on the one in Sydney, nodding at their shared history in so far

---

6. Pacione, "Urban Restructuring and the Reproduction of Inequality in Britain's Cities," 42.

7. Vincent, *Hope from the City*, 15.

as Sydney Harbour Bridge was modelled on the Tyne Bridge alongside the Sage), and which would provide a new home for the Northern Symphonia; and a new Millennium Bridge; together attracting millions of pounds of investment (both "public" and "private") with some ambitious hope—and constantly frustrated plans—as to how new moneys might by tricks and turns come to benefit the "deprived" local people. Note in the language of "regeneration," religious overtones, or at the least, a language that has religious currency if also biological meaning. As Robert Furbey points out, whatever the merits of New Labour's aspirations, their weakness was that such regeneration put the onus on the urban deprived to be regenerated: "Recent British urban policy, for all its seeming 'inclusiveness', utilises the idea of 'regeneration' within a restricted discourse. It rests on an apparently expansive and diverse, if not contradictory, amalgam of spiritualities, psychologies and social organicisms. However, its blend of individualism, conservatism, liberalism and statism invites compliance with a policy agenda that excludes perspectives and questions that imply change for the whole 'body' in favour of an emphasis on its most obviously dysfunctional extremities. It is the excluded poor, the alarming 'underclass' who are assigned the fullest responsibility to be 'born again.'"[8] Put another way, the point may be that however hopeful the rhetoric might sound, this New Labour-speak may simply amount to a twist in dynamics of what David Byrne calls "blaming the poor"[9] for their deprivation.

Interestingly, theologically informed sociologists—Furbey and Byrne, among them—were among the first to notice and critique the government's use of religious language. When their appeals were taken up by theologians (or "professional" theologians, more narrowly defined) one of the major contributions that came to be made was a call for a turn outwards from a focus on the regeneration-needy poor in search of a "whole-city" approach to rectifying social inequalities. So, Philip Sheldrake: "Theological reflection on cities in recent years has tended in England to focus largely on what have been called, especially in Anglican terms, 'urban priority areas.' This may actually produce an unbalanced result. If there are sinful structures of exclusion and social deprivation these are not limited to particular districts within cities but effect, or perhaps I should say 'infect' the city as a whole, both as built space and human community. If there is a message of

---

8. Furbey, "Faith in Urban 'Regeneration'?," 13; and see also Furbey, "Urban 'Regeneration': Reflections on a Metaphor."

9. See Byrne, *Social Exclusion*, chapter 1.

liberation and transformation that the Christian gospel proclaims, it must be an integral one for the concept of the city as a whole."[10] In doctrinal terms, Sheldrake's argument is for a kind of catholicity to come into play. Read together, the baptismal language of regeneration was being juxtaposed to—enriched, even corrected by—another theme in the so-called systematic agenda.

Sheldrake's "whole city" approach complements the lessons of the need for the greatest possible specificity, gleaned from following the moves towards sub-domains and geographical pockets in revisions over time in the Indices of Deprivation. The point is that on the one hand there is a need to focus on the very particular, whilst on the other there always remains a need to keep track of relation to the whole, so that local areas are continually seen in wider frameworks. The double dynamics suggest that a postal-code theology may best be developed in terms of oscillation from one optic to another: a locale—the postal-code—and its smaller pockets, but also its wider setting. This process of oscillation no doubt requires a certain patience, but a postal-code theology needs the constant re-focussing of these three as it were "intensities" of vision.

EXPLORING "PARISH"

In order to begin a second trajectory of reflections, I return for a moment to CA28 6TH. For a parish boundary ran down the middle of Highfields, so that the even-numbered houses on one side of the road were in the parish of Whitehaven, whilst the odd numbered houses on the other side of the road (themselves with another postal-code) were in the parish of Hensingham. In reflecting from that observation, it is important to begin by stating my sense that the idea of parish ministry as cure of souls for persons within a certain geographical area is not unproblematic. It might easily smack of attempts at incorporation, if not colonization. I note that the Uniting Church in Australia—the tradition in which a number of other reflections in this collection are based—has chosen to abandon the language of parish, favouring more consistent use of the language of congregation. And in other contexts, which have retained a sense of the parish, there is no doubt that the opportunities and possibilities for parish ministry are shifting. Yet I am struck by Sarah Coakley's sense that only on moving abroad did she come to "comprehend the special quality of th[e] low-key English connection of

---

10. Sheldrake, *Spaces for the Sacred*, 166.

prayerful 'presence', 'place' and ministry to the 'poor.'"[11] Her own reflections circle on the USA having "an entirely different spiritual sensibility from the 'rooted' one (however underacknowledged or despised) that exists in England . . . No 'established' church, no national parish church system, and therefore no historic link back to an originally monastic sense of geographical 'stability' . . . makes a difference of subtle, but enormous proportions."[12] Whilst the differences between the UK and USA are more commonly the focus of attention,[13] very little literature seems to explore the differences between the UK and Australia.[14] Are such differences relevant or irrelevant? In what ways, and who decides? Contemplating Sheldrake's point about taking a wider view, I am interested in what attention to parish as a particular manifestation of presence, might, in the interests of "catholicity," offer to an elsewhere.

Also, in noting the parish boundaries overlaid along the edges of CA28 6TH, I am not claiming the residents of these postal-codes as church-goers. Some neighbours, of course, were committed to particular Christian communities—at least Roman Catholic and Christian Brethren in the small postal-code, though none, so far as I know, to the Anglican churches whose parishes met at these boundaries. However, many sometimes as it were "by default" oriented towards the services of the Church of England, even if not in other ways allied to it. So, oftentimes neighbours were baptised, married or buried in different church buildings (perhaps consciously or unconsciously expressing "an implicit sense of national *right*").[15] This meant that socially involving life-events were focused in different directions; neighbours gravitated—or were pulled—different ways. In terms of the persons living in a postal-code, parish boundaries may have a significant impact on the sedimented identity of a household within it. And attention to parish boundaries might even be part of the "humanizing" of discussion of locales.

Also from the UK context is a descriptor from the Church of England's website, a "strap-line" for English Anglicanism at the present time, suggesting that it is "a Christian presence every community."[16] In urban contexts in the UK, the Church of England is sometimes the only old-line

11. Coakley, "Introduction," 5–6.

12. Ibid., 6.

13. Including in Heelas and Woodhead, *The Spiritual Revolution*, discussed below.

14. Frame, *Losing My Religion*, chapter 3, narrates the contours of early colonial Christianity and emerging Australian "irreligion."

15. Coakley, "Introduction," 14 (her emphasis).

16. Online: http://www.cofe.anglican.org.

church to have been able to retain a presence in the area—which may at its worst seem to suggest a certain triumphalism in the website line, but might more graciously be read as a signal of a dogged determination to retain resources in urban areas (albeit whilst still not sorting out other subtle and less subtle layers of inequality that clearly exist in the Church's life). It has also—so far at least—resisted the dislocation of its clergy from the parishes they serve: clergy *live* there. One of the remarkable things about ministry in some urban contexts is that clergy are sometimes the only professionals to both work and reside in an area of deprivation: to have perhaps closer and more sustained—but certainly particular—access to some of the factors that comprise the markers of the Indices of Deprivation. Whilst the services of the church were not measured in the government's "access to services" domain, nevertheless churches—wider than the Church of England—may wish to frame their ministries within the wider orbit of thought that the indices suggests. In the first place, as Sarah Coakley suggests, "Anglicanism's historic privilege to pastor the 'nation', and its simultaneous commitment to prayer, place and the poor, has now of necessity become a shared and *ecumenical* endeavour";[17] but more, in what follows, I am musing on how capacity for such a vocation might be fostered not only ecumenically but in other places.

In Britain, much of the recent analysis of the situation has been clustered through a trajectory begun with the *Mission-Shaped Church* report, produced by the Church of England in 2004, subsequently adopted by the Methodist Church, and spawning a series of further thought: books unfolding the "mission-shaped" aspects of say, Christian spirituality,[18] of mission-shaped manifestations of church in specific contexts,[19] or among particular sub-cultures.[20] It is claimed that "the ideas in the Mission-shaped Church report are taking root in a deep way across the Church of England and the Methodist Church and in many other streams and traditions."[21] Some of what has emerged in response to *Mission-Shaped Church* is, however, less loyal: John Hull's "theological response"[22] to the report was the

---

17. Coakley, "Introduction," 15.
18. Hope, *Mission-Shaped Spirituality*.
19. For example, James and Gaze, *Mission-Shaped and Rural*.
20. For example, Sudworth et al., *Mission-Shaped Youth*.
21. Croft, *Jesus' People*, vii.
22. Hull, *Mission-Shaped Church*.

first of several "mission-shaped questions"[23] and subsequent, less glowing, "evaluations."[24] Hull's critique is particularly interesting in light of reference to Philip Sheldrake's "whole city" approach to urban problems, cited above, for at the heart of Hull's critique of *Mission-Shaped Church* is that it in fact proposes a very "church-shaped mission," not aligned as it might be to issues of justice. In particular, he offers very strong resistance to the "development" of congregations in sub-cultural enclaves. One way to restate his argument might be to say that these forget the catholicity of the church. One implication in his criticism is that they may not just blame, but actively jettison, the poor.

Some of what has followed *Mission-Shaped Church* has been a trenchant restatement of the importance of parish ministry. Taking a longer view than the 2004 report, Nicholas Holtam nevertheless no doubt has it in his sights in his *A Room with a View*: "My sense is that a great deal of what passes for 'mission' in the contemporary Church of England is peculiarly inward looking. For the last twenty years we have been presented with a false polarity that gives priority to 'mission' over that sort of pastoral care in which ministers and churches cared for the whole parish and not just the congregation. It is difficult to know cause and effect, but in our anxiety to survive we are creating inward-looking, self-referential congregations."[25]

Holtam, then vicar of St. Martins-in-the-Fields on a corner of Trafalgar Square in central London, wishes to reclaim three aspects of parish ministry in particular: what he calls a parish's "openness to the world," "openness to the poorest" and "commitment to looking beyond itself" to God and God's reign.[26] Whilst "primarily . . . a 'eucharistic community,'"[27] there are nevertheless various ways in which persons can be encouraged to "belong to the church," "richer, more interesting and diverse than can be summarized by numbers on the membership list."[28] These include, in the first place, their service to a local community and the enabling of charity in that community. This is inevitably a broad category, defined by Holtam

23. Croft, *Mission-Shaped Questions*.

24. Nelstrop and Percy, *Evaluating Fresh Expressions*.

25. Holtam, *A Room with a View*, 1. In this section, I draw on voices aligned to my own convictions. Having drawn on my own 'story' in earlier parts of the essay, I have hereon resisted citing (many possible) anecdotes from my own experience in order point readers towards the established literature.

26. Ibid., 1–3.

27. Ibid., 5.

28. Ibid., 9.

in relation to the royal parable of Matthew 25[29] and rather vaguely as "love in action." But he also offers concrete examples, such as creating broad alliances to address issues underlying racism in a neighbourhood.[30] And a way in which the fostering of charity might take place in the church making available its buildings so that charity is "enabled by a hospitable eucharistic community" even as it helps to "to inform and educate that community."[31]

Other ways include the making possible of space for intercessory prayer,[32] the provision of some sort of education programme—and not just "Christian basics" courses, but the life of "well-informed discussion of difficult moral issues" like "a public meeting in advance of the war"[33]—hospitality to the creative arts, perhaps some sort of "honest commercial exchange" (in the case of St Martins, a café, for example), but in any case ways to open up "a place for the whole community": "Parish churches are important focal points in local communities. They are one of the few public places where people gather. As places of memory they also collect a community's history. This is an incredibly important function . . ."[34]

Holtam admits that, in St Martin's case, there is at times a "gap" between the aspiration he sketches and the reality of what is found, as anywhere else: "Every church says it is welcoming, but the test is whether the visitors bring anything that is valued, wanted, will change the life of the parish church and not just be assimilated into it . . ."[35] St Martin's-in-the-Field might claim a quite distinctive postal-code, alongside the National Gallery, looking across to Nelson's Column, a doorstep for tourists from

29. Ibid., 10

30. Ibid.

31. Ibid.

32. The feature that Coakley makes central to the church's public role: "without the *daily* public witness of a clergy engaged, manifestly and accountably, alongside their people, in the disciplined long-haul life of prayer . . . There is no *public* witness to the clergy putting this task first in their hierarchy of 'business'" (Coakley, "Introduction," 8 (her repeated emphasis).

33. Holtam, *A Room with a View*, 14.

34. Ibid., 18. Holtam then cites Simon Jenkins' Introduction to *England's Thousand Best Churches*, with "best" there related to picturesque-ness and the role of such buildings as "museums of England": "The local parish church . . . tells of 'homely joys and destiny obscure . . . the short and simple annals of the poor.'" In various ways, Coakley also stresses "the building's dense symbolic power" (Coakley, "Presence," 10), whilst other essays in the collection she co-edits—notably Stephen Cherry, "Representation" (21–41)—also draw special attention to this.

35. Ibid., 20.

across the world. Nevertheless, Holtam's depiction of the ministry of a local church might prod any postal-code theology to attend to the significance of the church's buildings within a particular setting, and invite attention to any possible ways in which permeability, as it were, can be enlarged between the "core" (Holtam's word) eucharistic activity within the buildings and other expressions of spirituality—in all their inchoateness, perhaps—and many other activities involving perhaps very many people.

Far from the heart of London, in the market town of Kendal in Cumbria, Alan Billings voices another robust defence of parish ministry. His is more theologically articulate than Holtam's and more specifically related—largely by way of contest—to sociological accounts of the increasing "secularization" of Britain. Billing's *Secular Lives, Sacred Hearts* was published in the same year as *Mission-Church Report*, and in some respects can be read as a head-on rebuttal of it. But it is also part of a more local contest, given that it emerged from a town which was the focus of Lancaster University's "Kendal Project," itself subsequently published as *The Spiritual Revolution*.[36] *The Spiritual Revolution* is a study of diverse expressions of spirituality in this particular town—itself a cluster of a handful of postal-codes—taking in both what takes place in the different kinds of institution in the "congregational domain" and the more diffuse "holistic milieu" that embraces a wide stretch of New Age understandings and practices, amongst other things. *The Spiritual Revolution*'s nuanced understandings of congregationsis itself significant, distinguishing as they do "congregations of difference," "congregations of humanity," "congregations of experiential humanity" and "congregations of experiential difference."[37] Broad lines that serve to sketch the distinctions include the first of these stressing the difference between creator and creation, the second focusing on the doctrine of incarnation and the practice of "service," the third a dynamic sense of the Holy Spirit, and the fourth a spiritual interiority.[38]

Kendal was chosen as the focus of the study because the demographics of Kendal are in many respects (except relating to ethnicity,[39] where it was more homogenous) "typical" of the broader population of England. At

---

36. Heelas and Woodhead, *The Spiritual Revolution*.

37. Ibid., 17.

38. In more traditionally ecclesial terms, all this might map on to the contours of for instance an Evangelical, a liberal Anglican, an Assemblies of God, and a Quaker congregation, respectively.

39. See Heelas and Woodhead, *The Spiritual Revolution*, 151.

least one of the researchers also lived in the town, when she was married to Alan Billings, a parish priest presiding in a "congregation of humanity."[40] And whilst not conducted under the oversight of the churches, many of *The Spiritual Revolution*'s conclusions are broadly consistent with versions of the "secularization thesis" that both charts and predicts the decline of institutional expression of Christianity, and which, in part, *Mission-Shaped Church* amplified. Billings, however, asserts that "the conventional analysis of Britain's religious health has never seemed to me to do justice to my own experience as a parish priest. I simply do not recognize what is so often served up as a sociological description of religion in Britain today."[41]

Whilst Billings affirms that "the inescapable message of the twentieth century was that the British people do not want to attend churches on a regular basis"—here akin to the understanding of both *The Spiritual Revolution* and *Mission-Shaped Church*—Billings is defiant that "there is no strategy of either evangelism or church restructuring that can make a significant difference to that"[42]—here launching a quite different tack to *Mission-Shaped Church*. Billings' own robust take on "the role of the church in a time of no religion" is centred on affirmation of "cultural Christianity":[43] the religion of persons who may "believe without belonging," albeit not necessarily along lines clearly determined by Christian doctrine, apart from rarely (perhaps, say, for a carol service or midnight mass at Christmas) engaging the regular ritual practices of the church. Billings locates such persons' attachment to the Christian tradition, such as it is, in "more emotional and practical than intellectual" modes,[44] and perhaps in so far as they are able to articulate it at all, in terms of the "golden rule": "do unto others as you would have them do to you."[45] He then turns to the ways in which such "cultural Christians" do commonly continue to engage the church and its ministers—

---

40. Linda Woodhead, with Billings the vicar of St George's. Whilst a parish priest, Billings, like the researchers for *The Spiritual Revolution*, taught in the religious studies department of Lancaster University. He had also played a leading role in the production of perhaps the most significant Church of England report in the twentieth-century—certainly the one to claim the most attention prior to *Mission-Shaped Church*: *Faith in the City* of 1985. Prior to that he had been Deputy Leader of Sheffield City Council.

41. Billings, *Secular Lives, Sacred Hearts*, ix.

42. Ibid., 11.

43. Such persons have variously been identified as proponents of 'vicarious religion' and 'differentiated religion' (ibid.).

44. Ibid., 18.

45. Ibid., 12.

at life-cycle events like baptism, weddings and funerals. So for Billings, it is not the Eucharistic "core" of the parish church's activities that is centrally significant, but rather the occasional offices. This, for him, empties *The Spiritual Revolution's* findings of importance, being "influenced from the beginning by the secularization thesis,"[46] it "measured Sunday church attendance but showed little or no interest in those other occasions when people come to churches in large—and sometimes very large—numbers. No one counted the numbers at Christmas carol services, for example, which have been increasing in recent years. No one thought that the occasional offices were relevant when measuring the influence of religion on people's lives."[47] In this contest, Billings can be regarded as launching his own "postal-code theology" against a pervasive perception of secularization. He is invoking the authority of local experience in the face of what he regards as a tendency to unsound deduction. And one of the challenges of his own inductively-shaped convictions is the way in which they can stir thought about public theology.

Consider just one of the occasional offices Billings explores, baptism or "christening"—the popular descriptor he prefers on the basis of its being popular—which, Billings asserts, may mean very significant things for those who seek it, whether or not what they seek is aligned to doctrinal understandings of the rites. He cites four reasons "why people want babies christened." First, they recognize that their child as in some way "an epiphany," and one which evokes "gifts"—his echo of the gospels' infancy narratives of magi meeting Jesus being quite intentional: "[l]ike the wise men journeying to visit the holy child, the guests at a baptism come to visit the baby who is shown to them, to express their love and to give gifts."[48] In seeking the celebration, so as to gather a community around the child for the event, it may well even be that the child's care-givers are in some way expressing their recognition that the gifts they seek are not simply material: "their showing [is] saying that human beings do not live by bread alone."[49] At the very least, the "showing" (a knowing connection with "epiphany" on Billings' part) is affirming that supportive family and good friends matter. Indeed, Billings' second suggested reason why people want their children christened is that the showing may be a very significant rite of passage *for*

46. Ibid., 126, n. 15.
47. Ibid.
48. Ibid., 49.
49. Ibid.

parents, especially perhaps when parents are not married, so that perhaps "baptism offers the couple the first opportunity to celebrate not just the arrival of their child but also their partnership."[50] Baptism may have "replaced the wedding as the couple's public acknowledgement of their commitment to each other."[51] The birth of a child may be understood to mean "the centre of gravity will now begin to move"[52] from personal interest to central concern for the growth of the child. Moreover, the child may commit the couple more deeply to their locality, as members of the household become variously enmeshed with its public services and institutions. In this context, a celebration in church is, in Billings' view, quite apt. Thirdly, Billings suggests that christening continues to be an opportunity for women to take control: "Baptism represents an opportunity for the woman to get her partner to something which many men are reluctant to do: think about the changed relationship that having a child brings."[53] Whilst some suspicion about designations about gender-roles and expectations may be appropriate here, Billings' claim that arranging a baptism is a way that women can take some control over their domestic situation still invites thought: "a baptism helps women to bind men more tightly into family life,"[54] just as in some circumstances it might help men to commit to their kin as well as to evoke the commitment of their female partners to do the same. For the un-partnered, christening may also play a very significant role for parents, enabling single parents "to assert their normality and acceptability."[55] None of the above meanings may much depend on the actual liturgical texts put to use in a service of baptism, though Billings' fourth suggestion engages a powerful symbolic act in the rite, as the child is handed over into the arms of the presiding celebrant for the moment of baptism itself. "The priest represents, yes, the Christian faith and the Christian community, but also the human community"[56] and handing a child into her or his (albeit momentary) care may signal an acknowledgement, at some level, that "each

---

50. Ibid., 53.
51. Ibid.
52. Ibid., 54.
53. Ibid., 55.
54. Ibid.
55. Ibid., 56.
56. Ibid., 57.

child born into the world is not only a member of his or her own family but the Christian family and the wider human family as well."[57]

Like Holtam, Billings appeals for churches to be "open." Without naming them as such—and of course nor does he mention "mission"—he raises interesting questions about possible meanings of public theology and how they might relate to attention to any particular postal-code. Billings has engaged what he perceives to be popular meanings of Christian traditions, whilst proposing that "church" is a complex constituency that includes, even welcomes, those locals whose views may be almost if not utterly heterodox from an "official" optic. At the very least, this points to the fact that whatever definitions are brought to an understanding of "church" are significant in any conscious engagement with "public" life, in any particular postal-code. As Dirkie Smit suggests: "What people envisage when they practice public theology is co-determined to a large extent by their *ecclesiological* and therefore by *theological* reasons and choices—be it consciously or unconsciously. It is on the strength of what people think the church is or should be, which in turn is based on how they think about God and God's purposes for church and world, that they form their opinions on what the proper public role of theology should be."[58] So whilst a congregation of difference (in either of the modes identified by Heelas and Woodhead) will yield one kind of sense, a very different sense may emerge from what Heelas and Woodhead call a congregation of humanity, and the ways in which understandings of congregations are juxtaposed to other—more catholic—descriptors of church will also make a difference.

It is important to claim neither too much nor little for what I am saying here. Whilst I am certainly not suggesting that the particularities of English Anglicanism are simply transferable to any other context, nor am I assuming that they are simply irrelevant to the situations in which churches in other settings find themselves. For example, among no doubt numerous relevant sensitivities to context, a major one in relation to reflection on parish from British and Australian locations is the simple fact that from the earliest colonial experience in Australia, and over time—at least outside Melbourne and Sydney, "where their lives were often intertwined

---

57. Ibid. Conscious that I have largely drawn on the reflections of male authors, I would also point to the importance of work like Clark-King, *Theology by Heart*, which is a compelling study of the 'ordinary theology' of local people, particularly women. It centres on a wealth of action-research focused on the parish adjacent to the parish of Gateshead, on the north bank of the Tyne.

58. Smit, "What Does 'Public' Mean?," 43.

with those of their parishioners"⁵⁹—clergypersons faced the very practical problem of sustaining even the most minimal ministry of pastoral visitation because parishes might be geographically enormous. But it is also striking that in a study of "unbelief in Australia," Tom Frame "cannot detect a uniquely Australian source of unbelief or characteristically Australian form of objection to theism."⁶⁰ Patterns of "complaint[ ] about religion" look to him to be much the same as in Britain and elsewhere,⁶¹ and many Australians appear to want some continued involvement in socially useful, if not institutionally involving, religious ritual.⁶² Frame cites annual Anzac commemorations that, amongst other marks, invoke a benevolent God, promote the "golden rule," "do not chastise" those who participate in them, and so in some ways can be judged to "belittle conventional religion." They are nevertheless imbibed with "Christian agnosticism."⁶³ There are, at the very least, resonances here with the kind of cultural Christianity to which Billings is appealing for attention. Neither christenings nor Anzac Day are all that mission means, but they might well be of some significance in local churches' engagement with wherever wider cultural currents point.

If the kinds of oscillation I commended in relation to postal-codes—smaller pockets and catholic vision—requires patience, as I suggested above, then the questions raised by my current explorations of parish no doubt require even more care. Not least in their questions of widely accepted secularization theories, the key point to absorb from the thinkers I have cited might be, in Frame's words, that "sometimes just discerning the right question takes years of reflection."⁶⁴ For some, there may be too little theology in whatever kind of postal-code theology I might be imagining, but in an arena of discussion of postal-code theology, I do want to read the different possibilities suggested from a particular kind of English experience as an appeal—although emphatically *not* a blueprint—that alongside postal-code, "parish" might somehow continue to make a contribution to a theology of the church and by the church. Whatever, *constructions* of

---

59. Frame, *Losing My Religion*, 45.
60. Ibid., 186.
61. Ibid., 186–87.
62. Ibid., 190.
63. Ibid., 190–91.
64. Ibid., 301. Entries on *clergy* in the index of Frame's book are all clustered in the early pages, as part of the narrative of colonial invasion. In the light of my reflections, I would be keen to see how further entries might be written into the closing pages of his book.

"church" and "world"—and of their relationship—play a part in configuring how mission and ministry are engaged in any particular place.

CONCLUSIONS

"My mind has been wandering," but I have arrived at some convictions. "Postal-code theology" is a valuable way of developing a local theology that can serve local ministry by a local church. The idea helpfully resists "generic-ism" in the practice of ministry which could otherwise be either a waste of resources or plain lazy. Postal-code theology can also learn ways to avoid making headlong mistakes itself: one is by zooming in to attend, by whatever means (I have cited the Indices of Deprivation), to specific pockets of experience within wider categories. Another is to zoom out towards a whole in which everything is connected—to let the notion of catholicity apply some pressure on local reality, even as the local is allowed to push back with its own demands. In these mappings, much is at stake in whatever is assumed about "church." At the very least, "parish" might perhaps have a helpful part to play—even though in some contexts it may need to be re-imagined or rehabilitated from near-death. But in my own contribution to a catholic conversation on local theology, I want the boundary running down the middle of Highfields to still whisper its questions among the several possible mappings to overlay upon a postal-code theology.

WORKS CITED

Amin, A. et al. *Cities for the Many Not for the Few*. Bristol, UK: Policy Press, 2000.

Billings, A. *Secular Lives, Sacred Hearts: The Role of the Church in a Time of No Religion*. London: SPCK, 2004.

Byrne, D. *Social Exclusion*. Issues in Society. Buckingham, UK: Open University Press, 1999.

Clark-King, E. *Theology by Heart: Women, the Church and God*. Peterborough, UK: Epworth, 2004.

Coakley, S. "Introduction: Presence, Prayer and the Poor." In *Praying for England: Priestly Presence in Contemporary Culture*, edited by S. Wells and S. Coakley, 1–21. London: Continuum, 2008.

Croft, S J. L. *Jesus' People: What the Church Should Do Next*. London: Church House, 2009.

———, editor. *Mission-Shaped Questions*. Explorations. London: Church House, 2007.

Department for Communities and Local Government. *Updating the English Indices of Deprivation 2004: Stage Two 'Blueprint Consultation Report': Summary of Responses*. London: Department for Communities and Local Government, 2007.

Frame, T. *Losing My Religion: Unbelief in Australia*. Sydney: UNSW Press, 2009.

Furbey, R. "Faith in Urban 'Regeneration'?" *Modern Believing* 42 (2001) 5–15.

———. "Urban 'Regeneration': Reflections on a Metaphor." *Critical Social Policy* 19 (1999) 419–45.

Heelas, P., and L. Woodhead. *The Spiritual Revolution: Why Religion Is Giving Way to Spirituality*. Religion and Spirituality in the Modern World. Malden, MA: Blackwell, 2005.

Holtam, N. *A Room with a View: Ministry with the World at Your Door*. London: SPCK, 2008.

Hope, S. *Mission-Shaped Spirituality: The Transforming Power of Mission*. London: Church House, 2006.

Hull, J. M. *Mission-Shaped Church: A Theological Response*. London: SCM, 2006.

James G., and S. Gaze. *Mission-Shaped and Rural: Growing Churches in the Countryside*. London: Church House, 2006.

Nelstrop L., and M. Percy, editors. *Evaluating Fresh Expressions: Explorations in Emerging Church*. Norwich, UK: Canterbury, 2008.

Pacione, M. "Urban Restructuring and the Reproduction of Inequality in Britain's Cities: An Overview." In *Britain's Cities: Geographies of Division in Urban Britain*, edited by M. Pacione, 7–61. London: Routledge, 1997.

Sheldrake, P. *Spaces for the Sacred*. London: SCM, 2001.

Smit, D. "What Does 'Public' Mean? Questions with a View to Public Theology." In *Christian in Public: Aims, Methodologies and Issues in Public Theology*, edited by L. D. Hansen, 11–46. Beyers Naudé Centre Series on Public Theology 3. Stellenbosch, SA: Sun, 2007.

Sudworth T., with G. Cray, and C. Russell. *Mission-Shaped Youth: Rethinking Young People and the Church*. London: Church House, 2007.

Sylvian, D. *Trophies 3*. London: Opium Arts, 2005.

Vincent, J. *Hope from the City*. Peterborough, UK: Epworth, 2000.

8

Displacing Theology
God-Talk in an "Age of Migration"[1]

Susanna J. Snyder

> Nowadays we are all on the move. Many of us change places—moving homes or travelling to and from places which are not our homes. Some of us do not need to go out to travel: we can dash or scurry or flit through the Web, netting and mixing on the computer screen messages born in opposite corners of the globe ... The idea of the "state of rest," of immobility, makes sense only in a world that stays still or could be taken for such; in a place with solid walls, fixed roads and signposts steady enough to have time to rust. One cannot "stay put" in moving stands.[2]

IN THEIR INFLUENTIAL VOLUME first published in 1993, Castles and Miller announced the "age of migration."[3] They pointed out that while human beings have always moved around in search of food, accommodation and

---

1. Note Castles and Miller, *The Age of Migration*.
2. Bauman, *Globalization*, 77–78. The perspectives and terminology in this essay were in process at the time of writing and are in dialogue with other more recent work. See for example, Snyder, 'Encountering Asylum Seekers', Snyder, "Un/settling Angels"; and Snyder, *Asylum-Seeking, Migration and Church*.
3. Castles and Miller, *The Age of Migration*.

work, the number of people moving across the globe, and in all directions, has increased significantly in the last fifty years. Contemporary migratory flows are distinguished by "their global scope, their centrality to domestic and international politics and their enormous economic and social consequences."[4] An estimated migrant population of 150 million in 2000 bulged to 191 million in 2005, a number the International Organization for Migration points out is "nearly two and a half times the figure in 1965, a pace of increase well in excess of the global population growth rate over the same period." Today, a figure of over 214 million is likely.[5]

This volume is concerned with how theology is undertaken in particular geographical localities—localities as defined by a certain postal code. It centralises context and seeks to ensure that theology speaks out of and into the reality of people's lives. A range of examples of what is variously known as local or vernacular or contextual theology are presented, illustrating that theology can never be understood as a "one size fits all" model. Theology or "God-talk" is not a set of concepts good forever and everywhere, but rather a complex, ever-shifting process of exploration and negotiation between theologian, contemporary context and Christian tradition. As Graham, Walton, and Ward articulate, local theology "draws attention to the specific form the Christian gospel assumes in any given place or time. It demonstrates that theology is culturally, temporally and spatially located, and that the gospel cannot exist independent of particular, embodied expressions."[6] Or as Bevans puts it more strongly, contextualisation is a "theological imperative."[7]

The phenomenon of contemporary migration poses some awkward questions to such an approach. Where do people who are "on the move" fit into a locality-focused theology? How might theology committed to contextualisation be undertaken in a global environment where hundreds of millions of people are travelling? How are Christians who are unable to claim a postal code or who inhabit more than one place to speak of God and understand their texts and traditions? This essay seeks to grapple with these challenges and point the way towards some potential responses. First

---

4. Ibid., 3.

5. International Organization for Migration [IOM], *Facts and Figures*; IOM, *World Migration 2008*, 2.

6. Graham et al., *Theological Reflection: Methods*, 200.

7. Bevans, *Models of Contextual Theology*, 15.

though, it is important to consider the nature of contemporary migration in more detail.

WHO IS "ON THE MOVE"?

Migration is a multi-faceted reality and patterns of human movement are infinitely varied. People journey in diverse ways and for different reasons. Some of us simply travel as tourists: we live and work at home, but enjoy escaping to a favourite island retreat or setting off to explore a new city or continent. Then there are those who travel for business, some for a few days at a time—scuttling between the London, New York and Sydney offices of a transnational corporation—and a number for more extended periods of secondment. Others choose to uproot themselves permanently for employment, often from the Global South to the North, in order to earn enough to send home remittances to support relatives and friends. While some move "legally," with official documentation and promises of work, many more travel irregularly, employing the services of identity-fraudsters and smugglers, and soon discover that they have no choice but to inhabit the underground economy and work for a minimal wage in the new country.[8]

Other individuals and groups have been forcibly displaced because of political persecution, civil war, social disintegration and/or environmental devastation. Legally-speaking, a refugee is someone who according to the 1951 UN Convention, "owing to well-founded fear of being persecuted for reasons of race, religion, nationality, membership of a particular group or political opinion, is outside the country of his nationality and is unable or, owing to such fear, is unwilling to avail himself of the protection of that country."[9] In other words, s/he has fled to another nation-state because of individual persecution. The term "refugee" has also acquired a more "everyday meaning" and is now more commonly used to indicate any person who has left his or her home because of political, economic, environmental or social danger and is seeking the protection of a new authority or state.[10] Some find themselves living in another part of their country of

---

8. Marfleet prefers the terms "irregular" or "informal" to "illegal" to refer to migrants who evade controls. See *Refugees in a Global Era*, 165. Use of these words—as well as "undocumented"—seeks to affirm that no-one is "illegal" and avoid the criminalisation of migrants who travel without papers.

9. United Nations High Commissioner for Refugees [UNHCR], *Convention and Protocol Relating to the Status of Refugees*, 16.

10. Sales, *Understanding Immigration and Refugee Policy*, 76.

origin—Internally Displaced Persons (IDPs)—and others in a neighbouring country, sometimes in refugee camps. Those with greater material and social resources often struggle via boats, planes and foot across thousands of miles to places with an unfamiliar language, culture and socio-political system where they may claim asylum. Asylum seekers are those who are formally seeking refugee status in a particular state but who have not (yet) been granted the right to remain there. By the end of 2009, there were approximately 43.3 million forcibly displaced people, including 15.2 million refugees and 27.1 million conflict-generated IDPs, as well as an estimated 12 million stateless persons worldwide.[11] At any one time, there are thought to be 2.5 million people in forced labour, including sexual and domestic exploitation, as a result of trafficking.[12]

Various attempts to typologise contemporary patterns of migration have been made. Collinson, for example, outlines a matrix based around distinctions between political and economic migration and voluntary and involuntary migration and Castles differentiates between highly skilled migration, low skilled migration, forced migration, family reunion and return migration. He acknowledges that there has been "a diversification, proliferation and intermingling" of these over the past two decades.[13] Bookman suggests that the two most significant differentiating factors are "duration of stay and freedom of choice."[14] While offering some illumination, such typologies are inevitably limited. Not only are people moving in infinitely varied ways (direction, length of stay, mode of transport etc.) but their reasons are also often complex and overlapping: political, economic and personal motivations are not always distinguishable—for example, civil war and poverty often coincide—and while some fleeing political persecution and civil war may enter a new country as undocumented "economic migrants," others seeking new economic opportunities may attempt to do so by seeking asylum.[15] The line between chosen and forced migration is also blurred.

---

11. UNHCR, *2009 Global Trends*, 2. "Stateless persons" refers to "individuals not considered as citizens of any State under national laws" as well as "persons with undetermined nationality." See UNHCR, *2009 Global Trends*, 23.

12. See UNGIFT, "Human Trafficking: The Facts."

13. Collinson, *Europe and International Migration*, 2; Castles, "Migration and Community Formation under Conditions of Globalization," 1151.

14. Bookman, *Tourists, Migrants and Refugees*, 28, 32.

15. For more on this, see Marfleet, *Refugees*, 121–24.

FROM TOURISTS TO VAGABONDS

A provocative set of metaphorical distinctions is offered by Bauman. In a postmodern world in which he argues that people are searching for an identity which is neither bound nor fixed, Bauman contrasts the strategies of the tourist, stroller, player and vagabond.[16] The tourist has a home but seeks adventure, freedom and amusement while the stroller only ever has superficial engagements and no specific destination and the player is time-constrained and focused on winning. He writes this of the vagabond: "the movements of the vagabond are unpredictable... Vagabondage has no advance itinerary—its trajectory is patched together bit by bit, one bit at a time... Wherever the vagabond goes, he is a stranger; he can never be 'the native,' the 'settled one,' one with 'roots in the soil.'... Entertaining a dream of going native can only end in mutual recrimination and bitterness."[17]

In a further development of this metaphor, he argues that our ability to move and the way in which we do so "has become the most powerful and most coveted stratifying factor" in the world and that while certain people can move whenever and however they wish, others "watch helplessly the sole locality they inhabit moving away from under their feet" and pay "more for the crowded steerage of a stinking and unseaworthy boat than others pay for business-class gilded luxuries."[18] The "extraterritoriality of the elite" is starkly juxtaposed with the "forced territoriality of the rest." He concludes: "The tourists travel because *they want to*; the vagabonds because *they have no other bearable choice*... The immigrant, travelling illegally and experiencing immigration controls, is the 'other' of the elite capitalist."[19]

There is thus a spectrum which can be outlined between more privileged and less privileged migrants. Some have many rights, carrying a universally-acceptable passport, money and visa and are able to visit any country they wish to while retaining a home. Others have little choice but to leave their homeland with nothing, only then to arrive in an alien place where they again face rejection, poverty and/or invisibility. People seeking

---

16. Bauman, "From Pilgrim to Tourist." For critiques of Bauman, see Coleman and Eade, *Reframing Pilgrimage*; and Tidball, "The Pilgrim and the Tourist." While "vagabond" literally comes from the Latin word *vagari*, meaning "to wander," the word has derogatory connotations and is thus discussed here with caution. It expresses the view that many have of certain underprivileged migrants.

17. Bauman, "From Pilgrim to Tourist," 28.

18. Bauman, *Globalization*, 10, 18, 89.

19. Ibid., 23, 93. Italics original.

asylum and those from the Global South moving irregularly to find work are among the latter. In the UK, which received 29,800 new asylum applications in 2009 (just over 3 percent of the global total), the asylum system is designed to deter would-be refugees, through the employment of stringent border controls, complex asylum procedures and detention, deportation or de-facto destitution when a case is finally refused.[20] One man from Somalia sums up the experience of many:

> Once you fail your case, everything disappears. No more housing from the government, no support whatsoever and this leads to stress and depression and suicidal thoughts. With nowhere to stay or call home, not being allowed to work and support yourself, the only thing left is to roam the streets and that's when one becomes vulnerable. I, for a couple of times, have been a victim of assault (violent), been beaten up for no fault of my own . . . We rely on handouts and charity organisations where available . . . Swear words and insults are an order of the day . . . Hope runs out and desperation, destitution, distress are all that is left. That's life for an asylum seeker.[21]

Other undocumented immigrants have to negotiate similar challenges, including no or limited access to healthcare, accommodation or food and no right to a minimum wage. They risk exploitation and abuse by unscrupulous employers and landlords who can threaten to shop them to the immigration authorities at any moment.[22]

STUCK IN THE MUD

While an exploration of the reasons for this treatment of underprivileged migrants lies beyond the scope of this essay, one factor is particularly

---

20. UNHCR, *2009 Global Trends*, 17.

21. Coventry Peace House, "I Came Here for Safety," 474–79. For more on the UK asylum system and its consequences, see Sales, *Understanding Immigration and Refugee Policy*; Amnesty International, *Down and Out in London*; Fekete, *The Deportation Machine* and three reports by the Independent Asylum Commission: *Saving Sanctuary*, *Safe Return* and *Deserving Dignity*.

22. For an introduction to some of the abuses which migrant workers in Asia face, see Baggio and Brazal, *Faith on the Move*. On the use of detention and deportation in the U.S. and elsewhere, see Kansroom, *Deportation Nation*; and De Genova and Peutz, *The Deportation Regime*.

relevant to the discussion.[23] Against the growing migratory trends outlined above grates the intrinsic need of human beings to be *placed*. We need to be rooted in a specific geographical locality with its associated sense of community and belonging and familiar language and culture. We desire, in short, to have a postal code. Pearson describes a postal code as something which "locates and situates us. The postal-code places us on the map and reveals telling tales of our neighborhoods . . . The postal-code option directs attention towards named and numbered environments."[24] It is noteworthy that one of the first questions we often ask people is, "Where are you from?" Location, place, home and country are understood to be revealing indicators of identity.

Inge, in *A Christian Theology of Place*, has explored the significance of place in Western thought and practice.[25] For Heidegger, an influential twentieth-century philosopher, the meaning of life lay in *dwelling*. Exploring the term *Dasein*, meaning "Being-in-the-World," he argued that to be human was to dwell—to be placed in a context with other human beings and material objects. According to Inge, Heidegger understood "placedness" to be "of the essence."[26] Casey has more recently written: "We are immersed in [place] and could not do without it. To be at all—to exist in any way—is to be somewhere, and to be somewhere is to be in some kind of place. Place is as requisite as the air we breathe, the ground on which we stand, the bodies we have . . . Nothing we do is unplaced."[27] A notion related to place is that of home, "home" implying house, lodging, safety, love, affection and community. We yearn for both place and home and one important focus for this yearning is the nation-state. While famously a myth or "imagined community"[28] and despite predictions of its demise in the face global governance, transnational corporations and flows of people, ideas and capital, the nation-state continues to wield considerable real and

---

23. These include fears of socio-economic competition and anxieties surrounding terrorism since 9/11. See Snyder, *Asylum-Seeking, Migration and Church*.

24. Pearson, p. 2 above.

25. Inge, *A Christian Theology of Place*. Place is understood, following Brueggemann, as "space that has historical meanings, where some things have happened that are now remembered and that provide continuity and identity across generations." See Brueggemann, *The Land*, 4.

26. Inge, *A Christian Theology of Place*, 181–89. See Heidegger, "Being, Dwelling, Thinking."

27. Casey, cited in ibid., 14.

28. Anderson, *Imagined Communities*.

ideological power. Belonging to a nation-state is still the conduit for and guarantor of human rights, nation-states retain the power to control their borders and in many countries, attachment to national identity remains strong.[29] In fact, the more that we sense that we have lost our place, home or nation, the more significance they come to wield. Elie Wiesel, a Jew with intimate experience of exile, recognises that the "longing for home" emerges *through* distance and estrangement.[30]

This focus on locality is, perhaps unsurprisingly, also found among Christian communities: they, like the rest of society, have a tendency to be "stuck in the mud." Most denominations have either a parish system—with the priest being responsible for the cure of all souls in a determined geographical area—or a network of local congregations, with ministers again concerned with those who live nearby. It has, for example, only recently become possible in the Church of England for couples to get married in a parish where they do not reside. Church structures tend to shadow those of the nation-state. The Church of England is found in England and correspondingly elsewhere, it is called the Anglican Church of Kenya or the Episcopal Church in the USA. Diocesan or provincial boundaries largely correspond with those of nation-states. Noting "the canonical stipulation that refugees become the responsibility of the local ordinary when they move into his territory from another's territory," Orobator points out that the Roman Catholic Church also "lays a heavy emphasis on territoriality."[31]

IMPLICATIONS FOR PEOPLE WITHOUT A POSTAL CODE

The consequences of this paradox—that though we are in a world of flux and movement, there is an increasing attachment to place—for the least privileged migrants are profound. Olwig and Hastrup suggest that our "place-fixation" has led us to see movement as a pathology: "The 'natural' state of the world was conceived of in terms of stability and social coherence; flight and suffering were out of order."[32]

Reflecting on the plight of refugees, Malkki suggests that their "loss of specificity" in terms of culture, place and history is held as threatening

---

29. See Joppke, *Challenge to the Nation-State*, for an introduction to the role of the nation-state.
30. Wiesel, "Longing for Home." See also Bauman, *Community*, 101–11.
31. Orobator, *From Crisis to Kairos*, 172.
32. Hastrup and Olwig, "Introduction," 6.

in a world where nations, culture, peoples and societies are assumed to be territorially bounded. She argues that refugees are liminal in this order and "confront [it] as a symptom of its own fragility and endangerment." They are usually depicted as "bare humanity," meaning "human in the most basic, elementary sense."[33] In a world in which full humanness is linked to nationness, "denying the nationness of an 'other' is denying its subjectivity." She points out that "in uprooting, a metamorphosis occurs: The territorializing metaphors of identity—roots, soils, trees, seeds—are washed away in human floodtides, waves, flows, streams, and rivers. These liquid names for the uprooted reflect the sedentarist bias in dominant modes of imagining homes and homelands, identities and nationalities . . . 'uprootedness' becomes profoundly unnatural, and perhaps the ultimate human tragedy."[34]

For the "tourists" who—while enjoying travelling—have a home and "nationness," the "vagabonds" represent what they may become: their uprootedness is what they fear. It is no coincidence that people who have lost much in the process of migration are known as dis-*placed*. Unlike migrants who inhabit two places or the "hyphen" between places, as Pearson puts it—those living in diaspora who retain a strong attachment to a homeland but have, at the same time, become rooted and made a new life in another—underprivileged migrants often have *no place, no postal code*. They become almost invisible to host communities and can be forced to exist in "non-places" devoid of established, shared meaning and identity.[35] Many have lost their livelihood, family, sense of belonging—at least temporarily—and sometimes even self-respect and hope.[36] Many have relinquished one passport (or never had one) and have not yet gained a new one. Destitute irregular migrants living underground, shifting from a friend's floor to a cold, damp concrete tunnel under a railway bridge, or refugees struggling to build a future in constructed camps miles away from home in Sri Lanka haunt the "tourists." They are their shadow side. Migrants

33. Malkki, *Purity and Exile,* 111–12. For a discussion of the different but related concept of "bare life," see Agamben, *Homo Sacer.*

34. Malkki, *Purity and Exile,* 257, 151–56.

35. Augé introduced the notion of "non-place," meaning a "space which cannot be defined as relational, or historical, or concerned with identity." See Augé, *Non-places,* 77–78. This is not to suggest that people seeking asylum and undocumented or trafficked migrants do not form significant relationships, find meaning or celebrate—it is simply to suggest that they do this *in spite* of the non-places in which they find themselves.

36. While discussing these challenges, it is also important to recognize that underprivileged migrants actively manage their experiences through a range of strategies. They are agents who make choices about where to live or work or find support, etc.

who have lost much loom as a spectre over the shoulder of their fragile placed-ness. They are, to draw on a pun of Freud, the "unheimlich" in the "heimlich"—the concealed, deceitful or uncanny in the friendly and comfortable.[37] Quoting Bauman again, in "the figure of the stranger (not just the "unfamiliar," but the *alien*, the "out of place"), the fears of uncertainty, founded in the totality of life experience, find their eagerly sought, and so welcomed, embodiment."[38] At a time when people are trying to hold onto locality, identity and belonging, the presence of migrants—and particularly those with few material resources and from places in the grip of violent struggle—can be deemed very threatening. They might "bring chaos into the social order" and in "numbers, they may come to be seen as a tide that will engulf us, provoking primitive fears of annihilation, of the dissolving of boundaries, the dissolution of identity."[39]

It is perhaps this which helps to explain why in 2001, when over 430 mostly Afghan unauthorised arrivals became stranded in international waters north of Christmas Island, the Australian government denied them access to Australian territorial waters. Eventually, most were taken to the islands of Nauru and Manus where they were detained for months while waiting for decisions about their future. The notorious Tampa incident—as it became known after the Norwegian boat which rescued them—reveals just how difficult it is for those who have no postal code to find a new one. Those without a place in this case were literally kept at sea, in the "non-place" of international waters.[40]

DIS-PLACING THEOLOGY

What then does this mean for theology? How should theologians engage with the experiences of people who have no postal code? Can they find a way to pay proper respect to context without becoming "stuck in the mud"? Theology, I would like to suggest, needs to be dis-placed: it needs to be dislodged and uprooted from its local "comfort zone."[41] The following section

---

37. Kristeva, *Strangers to Ourselves*, 182–83.
38. Bauman, *Community*, 115.
39. Sandercock, *Cosmopolis II*, 111.
40. Mountz, *Seeking Asylum*, 134. For more on the use of islands in migration management, see Mountz, "The Enforcement Archipelago."
41. Koyama calls for a theology "challenged, disturbed and stirred up by the presence of strangers." See Koyama, "Extend Hospitality to Strangers," 283.

points towards four ways in which this might happen—two ways in which theology could be disrupted methodologically and two tasks which such a dis-placed theology could consider undertaking.

Paying Attention to Migrants

Theology, firstly, needs to be dis-placed is in terms of its literal and metaphorical horizon. Currently, theological views tend to extend either to the locality or the broader nation, or they are abstract, disembodied views—understandings of God, tradition and scripture believed to apply to all times and places. Theologians (even if they are not theologians of migration) need to begin to pay significant attention to migrants and particularly to those described by Bauman as "vagabonds."[42] Despite an active presence in many church congregations, they currently fall just as easily into theological car mirror blind spots as they do through the gaps between nation-states. Migration is a pervasive reality in every corner of the globe and cannot be ignored in church or academic circles wishing to be taken seriously. Theology which consciously speaks out of and into migrant experiences is imperative.

This is not to suggest that theologies rooted in specific places are not important. They are, and the presence of a local faith community can play a crucial role in helping migrants to settle or simply survive in a new place. Churches, mosques and temples can provide an entrée into the local community and their local knowledge, networks and services sometimes offer a lifeline.[43] It is however to recognise that local theology needs to be done alongside a theology for the "postcode-less." The Christian tradition suggests that both landedness and landlessness are important vehicles for divine encounter. While on one page of the Bible, the virtues of being rooted in soil are extolled, one only has to turn over the page to discover an emphasis on the journeying of the people of God. Brueggemann articulates

---

42. It is interesting that a number of theologians currently addressing issues of migration are themselves privileged migrants, including the author. See for example, Phan, "The Experience of Migration in the United States"; Cruz, *An Intercultural Theology of Migration*; and Hanciles, *Beyond Christendom*.

43. See for instance Snyder, 'Un/settling Angels'; Levitt, "Religion as a Path to Civic Engagement"; Hagan and Ebaugh, "Calling upon the Sacred"; Hirschman, "The Role of Religion." The National Council of Churches in Australia offers resources to those wishing to offer practical support. See online: www.ncca.org.au/actforpeace/about_us/protect_refugees/.

this dialectic: "Israel is always on the move from land to landlessness, from landlessness to land, from life to death, from death to life."[44] God is with people when settled and "on the move," but significantly, it is when the Israelites become too comfortably settled that troubles tend to start. It is also often in displaced outsiders that God is most clearly glimpsed. Think of Moses, brought up by Egyptians and who married having journeyed far from home, or Joseph, an exile in Egypt, or Hagar, the Egyptian slave thrown out by Sarah and the first person in the Bible to whom God appears. Jesus had a special care for those beyond the vision of established society—for lepers, women, children and those with mental and physical disabilities. It should not then come as a surprise if God was to be discovered today moving in the "non-places" through which millions of unseen and unacknowledged migrants are tiptoeing and sometimes running across the world.

Paying attention and listening to underprivileged migrants is not easy however, particularly for those of us who do not know what it means to travel with little but hope or to find little but exclusion. Bedford notes that a migrant, "a speaker from a subaltern culture" who is rooted in more than one place (or indeed who lacks a place), "*cannot* communicate what he or she wants in" the terms expected by the dominant culture. Thus, "migrants can immediately relate to the question of not being understood because the persons to whom they are speaking do not know their origin or have the patience to hear their stories."[45] Not only do theologians need to tune *intentionally* into the frequency of the stories of unprivileged migrants, but such migrants more importantly themselves, need to be encouraged to share their theology. How might migrant experiences revitalise and reinvigorate established understandings of the Eucharist or catholicity or suffering or hope? What can underprivileged migrants teach others of God?[46]

---

44. Brueggemann, *The Land*, 12.

45. Bedford, "To Speak of God from More Than One Place," 108–9.

46. For examples of ways in which migrant experiences can challenge and re-define theological and spiritual understandings, see Goody, *Border of Death, Valley of Life*; Groody, "Fruit of the Vine and Work of Human Hands"; and Snyder, *Asylum-Seeking, Migration and Church*.

Theology "On the Way": Uprooting Mono-vocal and Mono-contextual Approaches

Attending to the experiences of migrants in this way also requires the uprooting of narrow mono-vocal or mono-contextual theological approaches. All migrants inhabit a variety of spaces, often concurrently, and are constantly finding ways to shift between different cultural, political, social and economic modes, assumptions and statuses.[47] Bedford notes how traditional understandings of the *locus theologicus* as Bible, oral tradition, magisterium, reason, philosophy and history have been added to by liberation theologians: they suggested that the poor in Latin America were the real *locus theologicus*. She argues however that the metaphor of *locus* or place for doing theology is fundamentally limited because of "its *static character*."[48] Playing with the notion of Gutierrez that we need to "drink from our own wells," she asks: "But what happens when those wells are left behind, in a geographical sense, in a place of origin far away? From what wells should *migrants* drink? Do we carry bottled water with us—or will the bottled water become stale? Do we drink virtual water using communication technologies—as when we read newspapers from home over the internet? Do we get inebriated on water from our wells when we are able to visit our places of origin? Can we dig new wells, and are they somewhat less hydrating by virtue of the water quality abroad?"[49]

She suggests adopting the notion of a *"via theologica* as a possible variation on the *locus theologicus*," recognising that for migrants, "the *locus* for speaking of God is structurally, by definition, a *way*" and advocates "learning to speak of God from more than one place."[50] Likewise, noting how immigrant identity involves being "betwixt-and-between," meaning "to-be-*neither*-this-*nor*-that, to-be-*both*-this-*and*-that, and to-be-*beyond*-this-and-that," Phan suggests a "multi-perspectival" "*inter-multi-cultural*" theology and Castillo Guerra argues for a "polycentric and intertopical" theology of migration.[51] Any theological work aiming to engage with and be relevant to the polyphonic experience of those who cross borders should

---

47. For personal stories illustrating these tensions, see Afkhami, *Women in Exile*.
48. Bedford, "To Speak of God," 103.
49. Ibid., 103–4. Gutiérrez, *We Drink from Our Own Wells*.
50. Bedford, "To Speak of God," 104, 112–13.
51. Phan, "The Experience of Migration in the United States," 150–51, 154; Castillo Guerra, "A Theology of Migration," 243.

make awareness of multiple cultural, political, social, economic and theological perspectives a priority. A range of voices—migrant and local, and diverse in terms of ethnicity, nationality, gender, sexuality and age—need to be brought into theological explorations wherever possible, and discoveries need to be continually open to challenge from new outsiders. Static and bounded approaches to doing theology need to be displaced by more flexible, conversational and fluid ones.

Task 1: Prophetic Critique

Such a new, disrupted, dislocated theology has two prophetic tasks. These arise from the two experiences of immigration identified by Phan—that of displacement and suffering, and that of being "betwixt-and-between."[52] One task, responding to the suffering of many migrants, is to offer critique and resistance. It is to grapple with the Christian notions of justice, love, neighbourliness, hospitality, solidarity and hope (among others) and on the basis of these, to call church communities, the public and governments to work alongside underprivileged migrants in order to transform their circumstances. Theology needs to lead to the denunciation of unjust immigration and asylum policies and systems, as well as to suggestions for fairer alternatives. It should also be exploring and exposing the connection between migration flows and the wider realities of global injustice. Much migration is a direct consequence of the fact that the "top 0.25 percent of the world's population have as much wealth as the other 99.75 percent."[53] In a world where place remains a crucial arbiter of rights and wellbeing, theologians have a responsibility to point out the need for all to access a postal code. Theologians should also be digging deeply into the Christian tradition in order to reflect on ways in which current ecclesial structures could be altered in order to meet the needs of postcode-less migrants better, and to highlight the importance of transnational and interfaith work on migration issues.

Dis-placed theologies seeking to engage with migration and the lives of migrants need, in short, to have a public role and result in practical change. As Min has argued, the priority of theology is "justice to the transcendent dignity of the other [which] entails the humanizing transformation of

---

52. Phan, "The Experience of Migration in the United States," 148–49.

53. Short, *Global Metropolitan*, 109. Castillo Guerra, in "A Theology of Migration," makes a similar point.

unjust systems and structures into liberating ones, and the mobilization of others in their solidarity at the service of such transformation."[54] Prophetic theology should be actualised in liberatory projects: there is a need for "stone beneath the sand" of theological talk.[55]

Task 2: Prophetic Vision

The second task of a displaced theology is imaginative: it is to offer a new vision of place in the light of contemporary migration. Theology needs to respond to the reality that many millions of people now live "betwixt-and-between" and move from place to place or "non-place." The task is perhaps to *re-place place*, introducing nuggets from the Christian tradition into a broader conversation around what "place," "community" and "identity" might mean in the light of enormous diversities in culture, language, wealth, mobility and religion. Envisioning is a crucial theological task. It is about imagining, and thereby starting to bring into being, a divine future.

Theologians could, for instance, dream an alternative to the focus on place as postal codes. "Postal code" implies the legality of a settlement and/or the status of an area: in London, an "SW" postcode speaks of white middle-England, Wimbledon and affluence, whereas an "E" postcode tends to conjure up images of multiculturalism and a mixture of deprivation and gentrification. Could a substitute be imagined which recognises the importance of locality and community but is also more positively attuned to mobility, diversity and statelessness? Given that in the Christian tradition, God is often known through the "outsider," a Christian vision of place could for instance be one in which migrants are able to bring and fully share their insights and gifts. A good place could be defined by its celebration of "otherness" and "newcomers."[56] In such a place, our first questions might be: "Who are you? What do you enjoy? How long would you like to stay here? What would you like to share with us?" rather than "Where do you come from? Why did you leave?" Migrants would be welcomed as a source of energy and gifts, and place would be classified and evaluated more by the

---

54. Min, *The Solidarity of Others in a Divided World*, 227–28.

55. Petrella, *The Future of Liberation Theology*, 145.

56. Castillo Guerra suggests that theology should aim to generate "a society of *convivencia*"—meaning the creation of common and harmonic spaces that make true encounter between human beings possible. See Castillo Guerra, "A Theology of Migration," 257, 262.

diversity and mobility of its human composition—by its *people-code*—than by the wealth or facilities it boasts.

The Christian tradition may also have insights to contribute to a search for identities not solely rooted in soil. Jesus disrupted understandings of the self dependent on the power one wielded in a particular locality, village or household and revealed the provisionality of all "homes" on earth. According to Moxnes, he transgressed and transformed place by a "vision of a new symbolic order" and created a "New Spatial Ordering—an Economy of the Kingdom."[57] Human identity was defined by the relationship a person had with God and how one treated vulnerable outsiders, rather than by an individual's "place" in the world. This understanding was taken up by and central to the early Church: Christians saw themselves as "exiles" and "aliens" on this earth (1 Peter 1:1; 2:11), moving through transitory, physical places on the way to their heavenly home (Hebrews 13:14). Müller has therefore suggested the metaphor of a "homeland of transients," drawn from Diognetus, as a possible new "ethical" identity for today. It "denotes a twofold movement: of openness towards universality and otherness, of true cosmopolitanism, but also of rootedness and faithfulness, of loyalty towards ourselves and ours."[58] What other metaphors or frameworks could be imagined and shared?

CONCLUSION

Displacement is an undeniable contemporary phenomenon and faith communities, including churches, are prominent among those offering grassroots support to those who find themselves without a place or between places. Churches need to continue welcoming migrants into their worshipping and communal life—celebrating their presence—as well as offering friendship and responding to requests for English language classes, social activities, housing, clothes or a legal referral. National and local advocacy on behalf of migrants is another crucial and ongoing aspect of practical Christian engagement. By contrast, in theological circles, migration has until recently remained the proverbial elephant in the room. This essay has hoped to point out the importance and urgency of acknowledging and

---

57. Moxnes, *Putting Jesus in His Place*, 106, 156.

58. Müller, "A Homeland for Transients" 145 (italics omitted). See also Bretherton, "The Duty of Care to Refugees, Christian Cosmopolitanism, and the Hallowing of Bare Life," 48.

embracing this elephant: it is time to respond to the theoretical, imaginative and practical call which migration places on all who engage in theological enquiry and reflection today.

WORKS CITED

Afkhami, M. *Women in Exile. Feminist Issues*. Charlottesville: University Press of Virginia, 1994.

Agamben, G. *Homo Sacer: Sovereign Power and Bare Life*. Translated by D. Heller-Roazen. Stanford, CA: Stanford University Press, 1998.

Amnesty International. *Down and Out in London: The Road to Destitution for Rejected Asylum Seekers*. London: Amnesty International United Kingdom, 2006.

Anderson, B. R. O'G. *Imagined Communities: Reflections on the Origin and Spread of Nationalism*. Rev. and extended ed. London: Verso, 1991.

Augé, M. *Non-places: Introduction to an Anthropology of Supermodernity*. Translated by John Howe. London: Verso, 1995.

Baggio, F., and A. M. Brazal, editors. *Faith on the Move: Toward a Theology of Migration in Asia*. Quezon City: Ateneo de Manila University Press, 2008.

Bauman, Z. *Community: Seeking Safety in an Insecure World*. Themes for the 21st Century. Cambridge, UK: Polity, 2001.

———. *Globalization: The Human Consequences*. Cambridge, UK: Polity, 1998.

Bauman, Z. "From Pilgrim to Tourist—Or a Short History of Identity." In *Questions of Cultural Identity*, edited by S. Hall, 183–86. London: Sage, 1996.

Bevans, S. B. *Models of Contextual Theology*. Rev. ed. Faith and Cultures Series. Maryknoll, NY: Orbis, 2003.

Bedford, N. E. "To Speak of God from More Than One Place: Theological Reflections from the Experience of Migration." In *Latin American Liberation Theology: The Next Generation*, edited by I. Petrella, 95–118. Maryknoll, NY: Orbis, 2005.

Bookman, M. Z. *Tourists, Migrants & Refugees: Population Movements in Third World Development*. Boulder, CO: Rienner, 2006.

Bretherton, L. "The Duty of Care to Refugees, Christian Cosmopolitanism, and the Hallowing of Bare Life." *Studies in Christian Ethics* 19 (2006) 39–61.

Brueggemann, W. *The Land: Place as Gift, Promise, and Challenge in Biblical Faith*. 2nd ed. Overtures to Biblical Theology. Minneapolis: Fortress, 2002.

Castillo Guerra, J. E. "A Theology of Migration: Toward an Intercultural Methodology." In *A Promised Land, a Perilous Journey: Theological Perspectives on Migration*, edited by D. G. Groody and G. Campese, 243–70. Notre Dame: Notre Dame University Press, 2008.

Castles, S. "Migration and Community Formation under Conditions of Globalization." *International Migration Review* 36 (2002) 1143–68.

Castles, S., and M. J. Miller. *The Age of Migration: International Population Movements in the Modern World*. 4th ed. Basingstoke, UK: Palgrave Macmillan, 2009.

Coleman, S., and J. Eade, editors. *Reframing Pilgrimage: Cultures in Motion*. European Association of Social Anthropologists. London: Routledge, 2004.

Collinson, S. *Europe and International Migration*. London: Pinter, 1993.

Coventry Peace House. *I Came Here for Safety: The Reality of Detention and Destitution for Asylum Seekers*. Coventry: Coventry Peace House, 2006. Online: http://covpeacehouse.org.uk/.

Cruz, G. T. *An Intercultural Theology of Migration: Pilgrims in the Wilderness*. Studies in Systematic Theology 5. Leiden: Brill, 2010.

De Geneva, N., and N. Perutz, editors. *The Deportation Regime: Sovereignty, Space, and the Freedom of Movement*. Durham: Duke University Press, 2010.

Fekete, L. *The Deportation Machine: Europe, Asylum and Human Rights*. European Race Bulletin 51. London: Institute of Race Relations, 2005.
Graham, E. et al. *Theological Reflection: Methods*. London: SCM, 2005.
Goody, D. G. *Border of Death, Valley of Life: An Immigrant Journey of Heart and Spirit*. Celebrating Faith. Lanham, MD: Rowan & Littlefield, 2002.
Goody, D. G. "Fruit of the Vine and Work of Human Hands: Immigration and the Eucharist." In *A Promised Land, A Perilous Journey: Theological Perspectives on Migration*, edited by D. G. Goody and G. Campese, 299–315. Notre Dame: University of Notre Dame Press, 2008.
Gutiérrez, G. *We Drink from Our Own Wells: The Spiritual Journey of a People*. New edition. SMC Classics. London: SCM, 2005.
Hagan, J., and H. R. Ebaugh. "Calling upon the Sacred: Migrants' Use of Religion in the Migration Process." *International Migration Review* 37 (2003) 1145–62.
Hanciles, J. J. *Beyond Christendom: Globalization, African Migration and the Transformation of the West*. Maryknoll, NY: Orbis, 2008.
Hastrop, K., and K. F. Olwig. "Introduction." In *Siting Culture: The Shifting Anthropological Object*, edited by K. F. Olwig and K. Hastrup, 1–14. London: Routledge, 1997.
Heidegger, M. "Building, Dwelling, Thinking." In *Poetry, Language, Thought*, 141–60. New York: Harper & Row, 1971.
Hirschman, C. "The Role of Religion in the Origins and Adaptation of Immigrant Groups in the United States." In *Rethinking Migration: New Theoretical and Empirical Perspectives*, edited by A. Portes and J. DeWine, 391–418. New York: Berg Hahn, 2007.
Independent Asylum Commission. *Deserving Dignity*. London: Independent Asylum Commission, 2008.
———. *Safe Return*. London: Independent Asylum Commission, 2008.
———. *Saving Sanctuary*. London: Independent Asylum Commission, 2008.
Inge, J. *A Christian Theology of Place*. Explorations in Practical, Pastoral, and Empirical Theology. Aldershot, UK: Ashgate, 2003.
International Organization for Migration [IOM]. *Facts and Figures*. Geneva: International Organization for Migration, 2011. Online: http://www.iom.int/jahia/Jahia/about-migration/facts-and-figures/lang/en.
———. *World Migration 2008: Managing Labor Mobility in the Evolving Global Economy* Geneva: International Organization for Migration, 2008. Online: http://publications.iom.int/bookstore/free/WMR_1.pdf/.
Joppke, C., editor. *Challenge to the Nation-State: Immigration in Western Europe and the United States*. Oxford: Oxford University Press, 1998.
Kans room, D. *Deportation Nation: Outsiders in American History*. Cambridge: Harvard University Press, 2007.
Koyama, K. "'Extend Hospitality to Strangers': A Missiology of the Theologian Cruces." *International Review of Mission* 82/327 (1993) 283–95.
Kristeva, J. *Strangers to Ourselves*. European Perspectives. New York: Columbia University Press, 1991.
Levitt, P. "Religion as a Path to Civic Engagement." *Ethnic and Racial Studies* 31 (2008) 766–91.
Malkki, L. H. *Purity and Exile: Violence, Memory and National Cosmology among Hutu Refugees in Tanzania*. Chicago: University of Chicago Press, 1995.
Marfleet, P. *Refugees in a Global Era*. Basingstoke, UK: Palgrave Macmillan, 2005.

Min, A. K. *The Solidarity of Others in a Divided World: A Postmodern Theology after Postmodernism*. New York: T. & T. Clark, 2004.
Mountz, A. *Seeking Asylum: Human Smuggling and Bureaucracy at the Border*. Minneapolis: University of Minnesota Press. 2010.
———. "The Enforcement Archipelago: Detention, Haunting, and Asylum on Islands." *Political Geography* 30/3 (2011) 118–28.
Moxnes, H. *Putting Jesus in His Place: A Radical Vision of Household and Kingdom*. Louisville: Westminster John Knox, 2003.
Müller, D. "A Homeland for Transients: Towards an Ethic of Migrations." In *Migrants and Refugees*, edited by D. Mieth and L. S. Cahill, 130–47. Cocilium, 1993/4. London: SCM, 1993.
Orobator, A. E. *From Crisis to Kairos: The Mission of the Church in the Time of HIV/AIDS, Refugees, and Poverty*. Nairobi: Paulines Publications Africa, 2005.
Petrella, I. *The Future of Liberation Theology: An Argument and Manifesto*. London: SCM, 2006.
Phan, P. C. "The Experience of Migration in the United States as a Source of Intercultural Theology." In *Migration, Religious Experience, and Globalization*, edited by G. Campese and P. Ciallella, 143–69. New York: Center for Migration Studies, 2003.
Sales, R. *Understanding Immigration and Refugee Policy: Contradictions and Continuities*. Understanding Welfare. Bristol: Policy, 2007.
Sandercock, L. *Cosmopolis II: Mongrel Cities in the 21st Century*. London: Continuum, 2003.
Short, J. R. *Global Metropolitan: Globalizing Cities in a Capitalist World*. Questioning Cities Series. London: Routledge, 2004.
Snyder, S. *Asylum-Seeking, Migration and Church*. Explorations in Practical, Pastoral, and Empirical Theology. Burlington, VT: Ashgate, 2012.
———. "Encountering Asylum Seekers: An Ethic of Fear or Faith?" *Studies in Christian Ethics* 24 (2011) 350–66.
———. "Un/settling Angels: Faith-Based Organizations and Asylum-Seeking in the UK." *Journal of Refugee Studies* 24 (2011) 565–85.
Tidball, D. "The Pilgrim and the Tourist: Sigmund Bauman and Postmodern Identity." In *Explorations in a Christian Theology of Pilgrimage*, edited by C. Bartholomew and F. Hughes, 184–200. Aldershot, UK: Ashgate, 2004.
United Nations Global Initiatve to Fight Human Trafficking [UNGIFT]. "Human Trafficking: The Facts." Online: http://www.unglobalcompact.org/docs/issues_doc/labour/Forced_labour/HUMAN_TRAFFICKING_-_THE_FACTS_-_final.pdf.
United Nations High Commissioner for Refugees. *2009 Global Trends: Refugees, Asylum-seekers, Returnees, Internally Displaced and Stateless Persons*, Geneva: UNHCR, 2010. Online: http://www.unhcr.org/4c11fobe9.html/.
———. *Convention and Protocol Relating to the Status of Refugees*. Geneva: UNHCR, 2007. Online: http://www.unhcr.org/protect/PROTECTION/3b66c2aa10.pdf/.
Wiesel, E. "Longing for Home." In *The Longing for Home*, edited by L. S. Rouner, 17–29. Boston University Studies in Philosophy and Religion 17. Notre Dame: University of Notre Dame Press, 1996.

9

Homemaking in the Diaspora
From Displaced Guest to Responsible Host

Seforosa Carroll

> Our existence as embodied beings means that our human experience is shaped by place.[1]

> I cannot help thinking that the Australian Aboriginees are perhaps right after all: that places define who we are, that we have no choice in the definition, that while we are not expected to stay in those places—we never lose our spiritual bonds to them and must return to them in one way or another.[2]

> One of the risks of leaving home is that home may never be the same when you return.[3]

I HAVE LIVED IN a flux of changing postal-codes and homes. On reflection I have always lived across various postal-codes, each with its own unique history and culture. Each in its own way has shaped and influenced my understanding of being at home and being displaced. My first home was

1. Inge, *A Christian Theology of Place*, ix.
2. El-Zein, "Being Elsewhere," 232.
3. York, *Pilgrim Heart*, 8.

Fiji. I am a Fiji born Rotuman. I spent my formative years growing up in Lautoka, the western side of Fiji. I left Fiji in 1987, the year of the first coup, in pursuit of further studies. My first postal-code on arrival in Australia was 2077. Hornsby is a suburb on the North Shore of Sydney. I studied for two years in 2031. Randwick is on the eastern side of Sydney. It is a two-hour trip from Hornsby by public transport. Getting to Randwick TAFE entailed catching a train to the city and then a bus out to the Eastern suburbs. For a newcomer to Sydney this was both a very helpful and intimidating way of familiarising myself with the vast distances between suburbs in Sydney. Hornsby and Randwick are two very different suburbs. It was like living in two different cultures in the one day. In a matter of two hours I would feel like I was in a different country. Randwick TAFE was host to many different cultures and people from all walks of life.

I did my Associate Diploma in Accounting in postal-code 2065. North Sydney TAFE was considerably different from Randwick in terms of ethnicity and socioeconomic status. I spent three years living and studying theology in 2151. North Parramatta was my first introduction to Sydney's west. While studying at the United Theological College I attended the Rotuman faith community (now a congregation of the Uniting Church) in 2047. Drummoyne Uniting Church was home to many migrant Rotumans. It was a place of both social and spiritual focus. I was married in 2047 and made my home (where I still live) in 2760.

St. Mary's is a working class suburb in the West. Its cultural makeup has changed considerably over the last ten years due to migration. Many of the shops in St Mary's town is now owned and managed by migrants. St Mary's is now part of the marginal seat of Lindsay. It was at least twenty years ago considered a safe Labour seat. It is now a swinging marginal seat.

I commenced ordination studies in 1997 and was ordained in 1999 in 2151. In 2000 I was inducted into my first placement in 2281. Caves Beach is a small beachside suburb of Newcastle of which the cultural makeup was then mainly Anglo-Saxon. It was also a haven for those who had recently retired. In 2002 I moved to 2134 and began my ministry as Chaplain to MLC School in Burwood. Burwood is a very multicultural suburb. Given the school's geographical location, MLC attracted many students from the inner West and as far as suburbs in the South such as Cronulla. In comparison to other Uniting Church schools in the NSW Synod, MLC is considered in terms of its student makeup to be both a multicultural and multireligious school. Over the last ten years 2151 has become a central location for me in terms of study, work and community.

On reflection almost twenty years later, leaving home was for me a search for home. Sarah York is correct in stating that "one of the risks of leaving home is that home may never be the same when you return."[4] I would also suggest that one is never the same when one returns home. The process of homemaking and being at home in any context requires a two-way process of shaping and being shaped by context.

Home is an ambivalent term. It can mean a range of things from a house, a street address, land, country, and religion, to feelings of security and belonging. In fact home is inclusive of all these things. My interest in home came about through my research on hospitality—or as I coined it hospiat*leity*, taking into account the oceanic practice of welcome symbolised by sweet smelling leis. In considering the hospitality relationship, I argued that hospita*leity* was a series of movements of which the ultimate goal was transformation of guest, host and space: that as guest and host engage in a dance of role reversals, spaces become endowed with meaning through the exchange of stories, which leads to the transformation of space into place. My fixation with home came about through reading Jacques Derrida who raised the question of whether hospitality is indeed possible if one is homeless, particularly as "hospitality is fundamentally connected to place—to a space bounded by commitments, values and meanings."[5] Derrida's question continued to haunt me prompting me to consider the notion of home and homelessness in terms of displacement and homemaking in the diaspora.

In this chapter I will consider the notion of home in relation to migration and displacement. This necessitates the exploration and unravelling of the strands which bind the migrant to the home of origin and home of new settlement (by migration or displacement). It also necessitates the exploration of the complex relationship between the body, identity, home, place, nation and space. The critical link is between body and space where the specific focus is upon the way migrant bodies are situated inside the national imaginary. Exploring the critical link between body and space offers numerous possibilities. It enables one to do several key tasks such as rethinking notions of home for the sake of constructing an embodied diasporic theology of home and homemaking. I will consider a theological framework for homemaking as a means for (re)creating "storied" places of meaning at both local and public spaces.

4. Ibid.
5. Pohl, *Making Room*, 136.

Home, as Fiona Allon states, is not constrained to the personal. It is also political. Allon observes "that home, now, more than ever, is seen as firmly connected to the world of politics and economics, as actively shaped and defined by the public sphere rather than existing simply as a refuge from it."[6]

Home is usually the site where worldviews, values and identity are formed and mirrored in relationships with "others" outside the home. A case in point is Pauline Hanson, the member for Oxley who made a deep impression on the Australian political scene in 1995 with her strong views on multiculturalism, Asian migration, reconciliation and Aboriginal issues. In her maiden speech to Parliament in 1996 she stated, "If I can invite whom I want into my home, then I should have the right to have a say in who comes into my country" (Tuesday, 10th September, 1996). Hanson is particularly interesting for a number of reasons. As Fiona Probyn argues: she is a white woman, who claims her authority on issues from her experience of being a mother of four, a sole parent, and a businesswoman running a fish and chip shop in Queensland, and who represents "middle Australia," "ordinary Australians," "battlers," "forgotten people," "traditional people," "people out there," "on the streets," "your average man, as well as people I have spoken to . . ."[7] Hanson has been described as the "Mother of the Nation" and has firmly embraced this descriptor leading to questions, as Probyn states, along the lines of what kind of Mother to what kind of nation will she be? As a Mother to a particular kind of nation Hanson draws the intimate connection between who is welcome in her personal home and in her country. In this instance Hanson exemplifies the embodiment of the structure of her personal home which is lived out in the political realm through her relationship with those particular "others" who, she claims, will not assimilate. In her maiden speech, Asian immigration and Aboriginal reconciliation, were for her policies that need to be reviewed. In an interview with *A Current Affair* on Australian television Channel 9 in 2007, Hanson latched on the latest immigration debate of reducing Muslim immigration.[8] What this highlights is that Australia's early exclusionary policy continues to influence current debates on diversity. The riots at Cronulla Beach in December 2005 raised questions about Australia's racism and strengthened the aging debate about the assertion of national identity. In

6. Allon, "Home as Cultural Translation."
7. Probyn, "That Woman."
8. Blunt, "Cultural Geography," 506.

this instance, Muslims were identified as a threat to Australia's social cohesion and were now officially the recipients of Australia's unique wave of hostil/pitality.[9] Religion had now become the new wave of racism.

Secondly, home is an ambiguous concept, that is: the meanings and lived experiences of home are diverse, incorporating: "a space of belonging and alienation, intimacy and violence, desire and fear, *the* home Alison Blunt states is invested with meanings, emotions, experiences and relationships that lie at the heart of human life."[10] (As such the idea of home [both as a metaphor and reality] and homemaking is integral to the task of Christian witness, discipleship and global citizenship.)

Sara Ahmed highlights three registers against which home can be measured or defined: country of birth, the address at which you currently live and the country you currently reside in.[11] In using these registers, Ahmed emphasises the ambiguous nature of home, highlighting that one could have multiple homes and that the notion of home is more than often affective. In this sense home is evoked by memory and experience. Hence, as Blunt suggests, the home is a space for both material and affective concerns, as these are shaped by everyday practices, experiences, relationships, attitudes, emotions and memories. Home, then, is not limited to a fixed physical dwelling. It is more than just a fixed geographical location on a map. It is affective and symbolic, thereby enabling migrants to inhabit multiple places at once. This, I argue, is the key to being at home in any context. It enables one to move from being a displaced guest to a responsible host. In order to make this shift, one is encouraged to engage in homemaking. Homemaking, as Iris Marion Young states, "consists in

---

9. Hugh Mackay makes the "tongue in cheek" comment that Australians have been remarkably hospitable to migrants. "There have always been outbreaks of racial prejudice against the latest wave—whether Greeks, Italians, Yugoslavs, Turks or Vietnamese." Mackay argues that Australians have long regarded assimilation as the key to a successful immigration program. Australians have assumed that migrants coming to Australia have been attracted by the Australian way of life, and Australians have taken for granted that migrants would want to enter into the Australian way of life as quickly as possible. Mackay observes that the traditional view of Australians to migrants is that they should become as invisible as possible and as quickly as possible. Australians have rarely spent time contemplating the difficulties faced by immigrants in trying to adapt to the Australian culture. See McKay, *Reinventing Australia*, 154–68.

10. Blunt, "Cultural Geography," 506.

11. Ahmed, *Strange Encounters*.

preserving the things and their meaning as anchor to shifting personal and group identity."[12]

Dislocation and displacement raises challenges and questions of home and belonging both at home and away. Spaces and places are not physically transportable. In the act of migration it is the memory of place and home that makes the journey across spaces embodied within the body. Bodies of knowledge embody within them the history, memories, stories and experiences of the home they have inhabited. El-Zein, an Arab-Australian migrant, makes this point when he says "I cannot help thinking that the Australian Aborigines are perhaps right after all: that places define who we are, that we have no choice in the definition, that while we are not expected to stay in those places-we never lose our spiritual bonds to them and must return to them in one way or another."[13] In embodying the places or spaces the body inhabits, the body also embodies the structure and experience of the home. Home is expanded to include dwelling or inhabiting at both the personal and political level. Although home is not limited to a location or a physical structure such as the house, "house" is often the first thing that comes to mind when one is asked about the meaning of home. According to Frederick Buechner: "the word home summons up a place—more specifically a house within that place—which you have rich and complex feelings about, a place where you feel, or did feel once, uniquely at home, which is to say a place where you feel you belong and which in some sense belongs to you, a place where you feel that all is somehow ultimately well even if things aren't going all that well at any given moment."[14]

But home is more than just a physical location. The home, as Buechner suggests, and as feminist geographer Linda McDowell notes, "in all societies is much more than a physical structure . . . it is a site of lived relationships, especially those of kinship and sexuality, and is a key link in the relationship between material culture and sociality."[15] To limit home to location and physical structure is to assume that home is fixed and immovable. Our experience as embodied beings shaped by place suggests that movement across spaces carries the memory of the place persons have previously inhabited. One such significant place is the home.

---

12. Young, *Intersecting Voices*, 154.
13. El-Zein, *Being Elsewhere*, 232.
14. Buechner, *The Longing for Home*, 7.
15. McDowell, *Gender, Identity and Place*, 92.

McDowell, drawing on the work of anthropologist Levi-Strauss, draws attention to the relation between house structures and social relationships. The point being that structural patterns within the household which are embodied in the body not only form who we become but influence and shape the "body's" relationship with "others" outside the home in the public space and even in the new space of residence in diaspora. Quoting Levi-Strauss, McDowell notes:

> The house and the body are intimately linked. The house is the extension of the person; like an extra skin, carapace or second layer of clothes, it serves as much to reveal and display as it does to hide and protect. House, body and mind are in continuous interaction the physical structure, furnishing, social conventions and mental images of the house at once enabling, moulding, informing and constraining the activities and ideas which unfold within its bounds. A ready-made environment fashioned by a previous generation and lived in long before it becomes an object of thought the house is a prime agent of socialisation . . . Moving in ordered space, the body "reads" the house which serves as a mnemonic for the embodied person. Through habit and inhabiting, each person builds up a practical mastery of the fundamental schemes of their culture.[16]

If, as Levi-Strauss contends, the body embodies the structure of the home, then the movement across spaces or a change in space or place will affect how the body may or may not feel at home. As Ahmed maintains, "being-at-home suggests that the subject and space leak into each other, inhabit each other."[17] Home is a place where one feels a deep sense of belonging and subsequently security, acceptance and connection. Home is the familiar, safe and comfortable terrain. It follows then, according to Ahmed, "that the question of being at home or leaving home is always a question of memory, of discontinuity between past and present."[18] The inability to feel at home in a particular place is related to the failure of memory and the body's inability to reconcile the embodied experience of home in the home country with the reality of home in the new context. In terms of migration, Ahmed suggests "that on the one hand home is a mythic place of desire in the diasporic imagination. In this sense it is a place of no return, even if it is possible to visit the geographical territory that is seen as the place of

16. McDowell, *Gender, Identity and Place*, 93.
17. Ahmed, *Strange Encounters*, 89.
18. Ibid., 91.

origin. On the other hand, home is also the lived experience of the locality, its sounds and smells."[19]

The failure of memory, however, does not always occur as a result of leaving home but is also brought about when the experience or memory of home is threatened. Ahmed states, "it is impossible to return to a place that was lived as home, precisely because the home is not exterior but interior to the embodied subjects. The experience of leaving home in migration is hence always about the failure of memory to make sense of the place one comes to inhabit, a failure that is experienced in the discomfort of inhabiting a migrant body, a body that feels out of place. The process of returning home is likewise about failures of memory, of not being inhabited in the same way by that which appears as familiar."[20]

Is the universal longing for home a yearning for the physical absence of what the memory of home promises? What is it about home that we long for? Is home, as Sarah York suggests, an illusion? And is it, as feminists such as Chandra Mohanty, Teresa de Lauretis, and Biddy Martin argue: "a nostalgic longing for an impossible security and comfort bought at the expense of women and those constructed as others, strangers, not-home, in order to secure a fantasy of a unified identity?"[21] Home is not only integral to the migrant experience. It is of equal importance to those whose home is being shared. By this I mean the host context. The nation as home becomes a contested space in terms of how space is shared. Questions of who is welcome, who is acceptable, who belongs, who is privileged and whose voices are heard and represented politically become prominent. In Australia the notion of home, or who can claim Australia as home, is measured against "values" and "belonging." Clemence Due and Damien Riggs argue that "in this context (*Australia*), the notion of home is frequently drawn upon in relation to both how people perceive the way in which they live, and others, belong in a country, and this raises questions surrounding who is legitimately able to call Australia home."[22]

The riots at Cronulla Beach in December 2005 strengthened the aging debate about the assertion of national identity or claims to home. The beach, which was at one time an image of Australian national identity,

---

19. Ibid., 89.
20. Ibid., 91.
21. Burkin et al., *Yours in Struggle*.
22. Due and Riggs, "We Grew Here, You Flew Here." Online: www.colloquy.monash.edu.au/issue16/due-riggs.pdf/.

becomes the site in which claims to home, by way of naming Australian values are being reinstated. In this instance, Lebanese Muslims were seen as a threat to Australia's social cohesion. The recent furore over the proposal by the Quaranic society to build an Islamic school in Camden is another example of contested space and values. This time objection was raised by a group of Christian churches (St. John's Anglican, Camden Presbyterian, Camden Baptist churches, and the Evangelical Sisterhood of Mary) opposing the proposal on the grounds that *they* were espousing views "incompatible with the Australian way of life."[23]

Iris Marion Young, in her reflection "House and Home: Feminist Variations on a Theme," makes a critical distinction between nostalgia and preservation.[24] Drawing from Martin Heidegger's "Building, dwelling and thinking" in which Heidegger identifies two aspects of building: cultivating (preservation) and construction, Young expands Heidegger's notion of preservation (as an act of remembering) to make the distinction between nostalgic longing and remembrance. According to Young, nostalgic longing is always for an elsewhere. Preservation is about remembrance. Remembrance is the affirmation of what brought us here. Nostalgia is what distinguishes a diasporic community from an established ethnic community. Unlike the feminists named above, Young believes that although their critique of home is justified she believes "feminists should be criticizing the nostalgic use of home that offers permanent respite from politics and conflict—but at the same time, feminist politics calls for a conceptualizing of the positive values of home and criticizing global society that is unwilling to extend those values to everyone."[25]

As home is a highly ambiguous and contested term, what then constitutes home? And what is the link between home and homemaking? For York home is the search for a place that feels safe and peaceful, safe from evil, safe from violence, safe from anxiety, safe from loneliness; no conflict, no division, no dissension. The quest for home is the need to feel we belong, the need to feel safe and the need to feel accepted.[26]

---

23. Murray, "Churches Oppose Islamic School."
24. Young, *Intersecting Voices*, 154.
25. Ibid., 161.
26. York, *Pilgrim Heart*, 40.

Further, Steven Bouma-Prediger and Brian Walsh in their book *Beyond Homelessness* identify eight aspects of home which they name the "phenomenology of home." These follow:[27]

1. Home is a place of permanence. Home signifies what endures over against what is transient.
2. Home is a dwelling place.
3. Home is a storied place.
4. Home is a safe resting place, where we are secure and at rest because of the mutual respect everyone has for the integrity of the inhabitants.
5. Home is a place of hospitality.
6. Home is the place we inhabit. It is our habitat and as such includes our non-human neighbours.
7. Home is a point of orientation. From home our world is made meaningful. Home is where we are loved and cherished.

Home is essentially a quest for identity and belonging. Home is a longing for what is possible but is yet to come. Home, then, in theological terms, is eschatological in nature. The etymological roots of "longing" share the same root as the word "long" in the sense of length in time and space, and the word "belong." To long suggests to yearn for a long time for something that is a long way off and something to which we feel we belong as well as it belongs to us.[28] This notion of home, identity and belonging is premised on the basis that home is not fixed but rather being at home in any space is dependent on the ability of the body to inhabit and reinhabit space.[29] It is the ability to create new spaces by transforming them into places (homes) endowed with meaning and value. In this sense home is like a journey as Nelle Morton understands it: a journey of gatherings along the way that has made what one has become. Home is not necessarily a place but rather a movement. For Morton, the journey is home. She writes: "I have come to know home was not a place. Home is a movement, a quality of relationship, a state where people seek to be 'their own,' and increasingly responsible for the world."[30]

---

27. Bouma-Prediger and Walsh, *Beyond Homelessness*, 56–67.
28. Buechner, *The Longing for Home*, 18–19.
29. Ahmed, *Strange Encounters*, 93.
30. Morton, *The Journey Is Home*, xix.

The movement is homemaking. Homemaking is not possible if one does not have or feel at home. It becomes possible when one is able to move from being a displaced guest to being a responsible host. In this sense, home is a basic human right that should be available to all. Young identifies four values of home that she insists should be normative for everyone. These are:[31]

1. Safety: everyone needs a place where they can go to feel safe. Home is ideally a safe place.
2. Individuation: to have a proper existence, individuals require a home, a space they can call their own.
3. Privacy: a people or persons is entitled to their own private space. To own a space is to have autonomy over admission to the space and contents.
4. Preservation: home is the site of construction and reconstruction of one's self.

The act of homemaking is further expanded by Rabbi Jonathan Sacks, Chief Rabbi of the United Hebrew Congregations of Britain and the Commonwealth. Rabbi Sacks uses the following three metaphors to describe the multicultural policies of the United Kingdom. In the metaphor of society as country house, the code of hospitality is that you are welcome as a guest; however, the host will always remain the host. In the metaphor of society as a hotel, relationship between guests and hosts is contractual. Services are paid for. There is no sense of belonging or loyalty. All (guest and host) remain strangers and sojourners. It is the metaphor of society as home that offers the greatest promise. This metaphor suggests a strong, mutual connection to place, whereby newcomers invest their energies in what they build. They are shaped by what they build and invest in, as it embodies something of who they are. The "homes they build are recognizably of the place where they are, not the place they have come from. Not only have they made a home, they have made themselves at home, in this landscape, this setting, this place."[32]

Homemaking is the task we are entrusted with in order to make the idea of home possible. It is creating and recreating spaces/places into meaningful shared storied places. The activities of preservation of the meaningful

---

31. Young, *Intersecting Voices*, 161–64.
32. Sacks, *The Home We Build Together*, 13–23.

things that constitute home are important both as personal and communal or public acts. Homemaking is a shared task. It is inclusive of women and men.

According to Robert Ginsberg, human beings are "home-makers." He writes: "We make our homes. Not necessarily by constructing them, although some people do that. We build the intimate shell of our lives by the organization and furnishing of space in which we live. How we function as persons is linked to how we make ourselves at home. We need time to make our dwelling into a home . . . Our residence is where we live, but our home is how we live."[33]

Homemaking is a process of creating a *habitus* for meaningful inhabitation[34] whereby the *oikos*, the economy or household is founded on the values of hospitality, dialogue, reconciliation, compassion, and justice where both human and non-human life is nourished. Inhabitation is a matter of embodied being. It is a two way street, whereby we are shaped by place and place is shaped by the relationship we have with it. It is, as Ahmed states, "body and place leak into each other." Being at home is a process of inhabitation. As home is fundamentally a place of connection, of relationships that are life-giving and foundational, and that include the past, homemaking, as Young describes it, "consists in the activities of endowing things with living meaning, arranging them in space in order to facilitate the life activities of those to whom they belong, and preserving them, along with their meaning which is both a personal and collective act of identity. Homemaking is a redemptive act of story telling which in turn requires us to restructure the household by the symbols we choose to identify ourselves by."[35]

Homemaking requires the movement of being a displaced guest to that of being a responsible host. The challenge is providing a framework and an open environment that can help facilitate dialogue and strengthen relationships. The metaphor of home and homemaking provides, I believe, a possibility of deepening relationships that may in turn open up new ways of speaking, listening, and acting.

---

33. Ginsberg, "Meditations on Homelessness and Being at Home," 31.
34. Bouma-Prediger and Walsh, *Beyond Homelessness*.
35. Young, *Intersecting Voices*, 151.

WORKS CITED

Ahmed, S. *Strange Encounters: Embodied Others in Post-Coloniality*. Trans-formations. London: Routledge, 2000.

Allon, F. "Home as Cultural Translation: John Howard's Earlwood." *Communal/Plural* 5 (1997) 1–13.

Buechner, F. *The Longing for Home: Recollections and Reflections*. San Francisco: HarperSanFrancisco, 1996.

Blunt, A. "Cultural Geography: Cultural Geographies of Home." *Progress in Human Geography* 29 (2005) 505–15.

Bouma-Prediger, S., and B. J. Walsh. *Beyond Homelessness: Christian Faith in a Culture of Displacement*. Grand Rapids: Eerdmans, 2008.

Burkin, E. et al. *Yours in Struggle: Three Feminist Perspectives on Anti-Semitism and Racism*. Ithaca, NY: Firebrand, 1988.

Due, C., and D. Riggs. "We Grew Here, You Flew Here: Claims to Home in the Cronulla Riots." *Colloquy* 16 (2008) 210–28. Online: http://arts.monash.edu.au/ecps/colloquy/journal/issue016/due-riggs.pdf.

El-Zein, A. "Being Elsewhere: On Longing and Belonging." In *Arab-Australians Today: Citizenship and Belonging*, edited by G. Hage, 225–40. Carlton South: Melbourne University Press, 2002.

Ginsberg, R. "Meditations on Homelessness and Being at Home: In the Form of a Dialogue." In *The Ethics of Homelessness: Philosophical Perspectives*, edited by J. M. Abbarno, 29–40. Value Inquiry Book Series 86. Amsterdam: Rodopi, 1999.

Inge, J. *A Christian Theology of Place*. Explorations in Practical, Pastoral, and Empirical Theology. Aldershot, UK: Ashgate, 2003.

McDowell, L. *Gender, Identity and Place: Understanding Feminist Geographies*. Cambridge, UK: Polity, 1999.

McKay, H. *Reinventing Australia: The Mind and Mood of Australia in the 90s*. Sydney: Angus & Robertson, 1993.

Morton, N. *The Journey Is Home*. Boston: Beacon, 1985.

Murray, E. "Churches Oppose Islamic School." *Sydney Morning Herald*, April 22, 2009. Online: http://www.smh.com.au/national/churches-oppose-islamic-school-20090421-ae1i.html/.

Pohl, C. D. *Making Room: Recovering Hospitality as a Christian Tradition*. Grand Rapids: Eerdmans, 1999.

Probyn, F. "That Woman: Hanson and Cultural Crisis." *Australian Feminist Studies* 29 (1999) 161–71.

Sacks, J. *The Home We Build Together: Recreating Society*. London: Continuum, 2007.

York, S. *Pilgrim Heart: The Inner Journey Home*. San Francisco: Jossey-Bass, 2001.

Young, I. M. *Intersecting Voices: Dilemmas of Gender, Political Philosophy and Policy*. Princeton: Princeton University Press, 1997.

10

Crossing Postal-Codes in Early Modern Japan

The Stories of Tamura Naomi and Osaka Motokichiro

Thomas Hastings

IN THIS ESSAY, I will briefly present the case studies of Tamura Naomi (1858–1934), and Osaka Motokichiro (1880–1945), two Japanese Protestant pastors who had the rare opportunity to study in the United States early on in their careers. Crossing over the vastly different postal codes of Japan and the United States, Tamura and Osaka and their churches, who were just beginning to transition from being "missionary churches" to being "indigenous churches," were caught up in what Sanneh calls the dynamics of relativization and destigmatization.[1] In addition to the modernist modes of thinking and discourse they had learned in North America, Tamura and Osaka naturally continued to reflect their native Confucian *habitus* that seeks to blend a harmonious personal integration of reason, emotion, and volition with a strong sense of public duty and engagement. It is precisely this personal-social, embodied conflict between modernist and traditional epistemologies that is the creative

---

1. Sanneh, *Translating the Message*.

basis of their work. In both cases, these tensions engendered pendulous ideological shifts. Tamura's ideological convictions evolved from a more orthodox evangelicalism to a publicly engaged liberalism while Osaka moved from a more publicly oriented liberalism to a mystical ancient catholic orthodoxy. It is my hope that these perilous theo-political narratives from modern Japan might be some help to those who are attempting to sort out the challenges and opportunities of the increasing religious and cultural pluralism within and beyond our various postal codes.

FROM ORTHODOXY TO LIBERALISM

Tamura Naomi was born into the Asaba family in 1858 and later adopted by another wealthier samurai family named Tamura, he moved to Tokyo in 1873 where he studied English with Presbyterian missionary Miss Park. Baptized in 1874 by Presbyterian missionary J. Carrothers, Tamura attended the missionary-run seminary and was ordained in 1879 as the first native pastor of the First Presbyterian Church in Tokyo. Tamura studied theology at Auburn and Princeton seminaries (first Japanese graduate, class of 1886) and psychology at Princeton University from 1882 to 1886. In 1893, two years after Uchimura Kanzo's well-known *Lese Majesty Incident*, a forgotten but perhaps even more significant incident in the history of Japanese Christianity took place involving Tamura and his recently established church, the Church of Christ in Japan (Presbyterian). In 1886, just after returning from the United States with a joint Master's degree from Princeton Theological Seminary and Princeton University, Tamura published a small book in Japanese called *Beikoku no Fujin (American Women)* which criticized what he perceived to be the miserable plight of Japanese women in light of the much more favorable situation of women he had witnessed firsthand in the United States. Flowing from his normative understanding of Christian social ethics at the time, the book advocated equal rights for women and men and urged the need for the construction of a new kind of family in Japan. Tamura believed that this familial ideal, in which the faithfulness of both men and women would be maintained, and through which the social status of women would be improved, was only possible by the power of Christianity.[2] Very much in keeping with the spirit of the age of Westernization described above, *Beikoku no Fujin* was evidently well

---

2. Naomi, *Fifty Years of Faith*, 208.

received inside and outside the Japanese churches.³ According to Tamura's own account, not a single person "raised any questions about the content of the book nor about his personal character."⁴

However, after returning from a trip to the United States in 1892 to raise money for his boarding house for poor students (*Jieikan*),⁵ Tamura slightly revised his *Beikoku no Fujin* for an English audience with the help of a classmate from Auburn Theological Seminary. The book was published in English in 1893 by Harper & Brothers as *The Japanese Bride*.⁶ Recounting the events that unfolded subsequent to the English publication, Tamura wrote that he had been ominously forewarned by his missionary friend David Thompson⁷ not to go through with the publication. "When he heard that this book was going to be published in the United States, Thompson visited my home and told me, 'In the current situation, to clearly reveal the Japanese situation in an English writing would not only be a dangerous but an unwise action. For your own safety, I think it would be best to abandon the idea.'"⁸

While expressing his gratitude for Thompson's kind concern, Tamura reportedly told him that he was convinced of his duty as a Christian and lover of the truth to speak openly about the shortcomings of the Japanese, even if he had to endure the world's attack.⁹ The eight chapters of *The Japanese Bride* are titled as follows: (1) "Why Do We Marry?"; (2) "Courting"; (3) "The Go-Between"; (4) "Preparation for the Wedding"; (5) "The

---

3. For example, leading Meiji Era educator Fukuzawa Yukichi had written a similar critique of the situation of Japanese women in *Japanese Women* (*Nihon no Fujinron*, 1885) and *New Women's Education* (*Shin Joshi Daigaku*, 1889). While he said that the family was hell for the Japanese women, and called for their liberation, Takeda Kiyoko points out that Fukuzawa wrote those books for the male students at his Keio College: Kiyoko, *The Yohohama Band's View of Women*, 9.

4. Enns, "Slander against Our People," 21.

5. In 1894, Tamura opened the Jieikan as a self-supporting boarding house for impoverished students. After its name was changed to the Tamura Juku in 1904, it remained in operation until 1919. One list of forty-one former Jieikan boarders includes six teachers, two painters, a philosophy professor, a veterinarian, two bankers, a physics professor, a history professor, a composer, a lawyer, a pastor and professor of theology, an employee of Japan Steamship Company, a member of the government's communications bureau. *Research on the Tsukiji Band*, 134–39.

6. Naomi, *The Japanese Bride*.

7. Thompson was a missionary of the Presbyterian Church in the U.S.A. and husband of Mary Park, Tamura's former English teacher.

8. Tamura, *Fifty Years of Faith*, 211–12.

9. Ibid.

Wedding Ceremony"; (6) "The Honey-Moon"; (7) "Bride and Bridegroom at Home"; and (8) "Mother and Grandmother." Takeda Kiyoko summarizes the central points of Tamura's critique of the Japanese family system.

Because marriage in Japan is not based on love but on the importance of the succession of family lineage, girls are taught from a young age that they are inferior to boys, their marriages are decided by their parents and thus afford them no opportunity for personal relations with the opposite sex, they go from being the property of their father to being their husband's property, and, like the relation between an absolute monarch and his subjects, the wife is expected to be absolutely obedient to her husband. Even if the husband engages in immoral relations with a geisha or another woman, the wife should never resist but rather bear it patiently with a smile. Disobedience to her husband or mother-in-law immediately means divorce. The husband can obtain a divorce according to his own wishes, but the wife has no rights whatsoever. Obedience is the paramount virtue in Japan. Without the efforts of Christians, the Japanese will never be able to taste true love.[10] Takeda points out that, ironically fifty-two years later, it was exactly the same issues which Tamura had raised in *The Japanese Bride* that were once again subject to sharp criticism in the aftermath of Japan's defeat in World War II.[11]

Thus, the book represents a prescient if somewhat politically naive critique, from the normative ethical perspective of a first generation Japanese Christian, of Japanese marriage customs that Tamura judged to be oppressive and antithetical to Christian faith. In the Preface, he justifies this direct critical approach by offering his own interpretation of the above-described situation in the 1890s. I will quote it at length.

> This is the age of danger and the age of confusion with Japan. Old Japan is passing away, and new Japan is coming to the threshold. The old man's opinion is no longer respected, and the young man's word has no weight. Buddhism, Shintoism, and Confucianism have lost their power of control, and Christianity has not yet taken hold of the mass of our people. Old and new customs are mingled together, and they do not work well. Old men are content to marry in accordance with old customs, but young men wish to marry in the foreign way, making their own choice of a wife, yet without moral restraint, although they breathe the air of new thought imported from Christian countries. Young men are dissatisfied with

10. Takeda, *The Yohohama Band's View of Women*, 9.
11. Ibid., 10.

old customs of marriage, but they cannot easily adopt a new mode
... This shows something of the result of the confusion of old and
new, and the danger to our inner life in this transition period. You
might ask, on reading my book on "The Japanese Bride," Is not
there a noble virtue in woman's obedience, in such a solemnity at
the wedding ceremony, and in such warm devotion of young men
towards their old parents? Yes, indeed! But Japanese virtue is very
pharisaical—in form, not in heart. Nine out of ten ladies in Japan obey their husbands not joyfully, but unwillingly, just like the
people of an absolute monarch. Our wedding solemnity does not
indicate the purity of our hearts, or the sacredness of the marriage
institution. I have frankly painted our home life which foreigners never penetrate, and which most Japanese hesitate to reveal,
feeling it to be a shame to open the dark side of our home life in
public, and especially before the gaze of foreigners. I have tried to
write with sincerity, in the spirit of loving truth, without any fear.[12]

While Tamura's rhetoric anticipates a strong reaction from some readers, he had no idea that his little book, ostensibly written "with sincerity, in the spirit of loving truth, without any fear," would create such a huge stir, not only outside but also inside the Japanese church. For a brief period of time, Tamura became a household name.

By the fall of 1893, Tamura's book had become the subject of harsh criticism, with over 200 Japanese newspapers covering the story. Tamura was accused of sullying Japanese virtue and the government even outlawed the retranslation of the book back into Japanese.[13] Tamura received some death threats from irate ultranationalists that he magnanimously laughed off, but there are reports that the boarders at his Jieikan stood guard for him at night with bamboo sticks.

These developments worsened the predicament of the already fledgling Japanese churches. With the recollection of Uchimura's refusal to bow before the Rescript still fresh in the public's mind, Tamura's book added fuel to the growing sentiment that Christianity was clearly irreconcilable with Japan's nationalist aspirations. Japanese society had undergone a decisive change of direction between the publication of *Beikoku no Fujin* and *The Japanese Bride*. As Tamura and others were touting the more amicable situation of American marriages, the Japanese family was being reinvented to serve nationalist ends. In its Civil Code (1896), the Meiji Government

---

12. Tamura, *The Japanese Bride*, iii–v.
13. Furuya and Ohki, *A Theology of Japan*, 122.

in effect universalized the traditional samurai family, the *ie*, by granting absolute authority to the head of the household and subordinating all other family members under a strict patriarchal lineage. But the "modern" Meiji *ie* system differed in one significant way from its Tokugawa Era predecessor. Rather than subordinating household heads to the authority of the local lord, village community or trade associations as during the Tokugawa period, the Meiji *ie* was re-fashioned into the basic unit of the modern Japanese nation-state of which the emperor was the inviolable patriarchal head. Nishikawa Yuko writes, "Japan, indeed, was said to have a unique system called the "family state," as witnessed in the Imperial Rescript on Education of 1890, which defined the nation as an extended form of an *ie*."[14]

It did not take long for the winds of suspicion stirring among the public to blow across the threshold of the churches. Uemura Masahisa, Tamura's boyhood friend and emerging leader of the Japanese Presbyterians, who had himself often expressed progressive views on marriage and the family, was the first Christian leader to publish a sharp critique of Tamura and his book on August 18, 1893.[15] Next, an investigative committee of the Tokyo Presbytery of the Church of Christ in Japan (Presbyterian) presented its findings on Tamura's case at a meeting on October 5, 1893. Outlining the points that they found especially offensive, the three-person committee, all former associates of Tamura, charged him with "slandering the people" (*dohozambuzai*) and demanded he "publish, in the near future, an appropriate retraction in five magazines and newspapers in Japan and America."[16] In language that reflected almost word for word the critique of the nationalist newspapers, one of the committee members summarized the Presbytery's concerns as follows: "The main point is that as a result of this book Mr. Tamura has slandered the 40 million people of Japan. He has damaged the integrity and defamed the honor of our imperial Japan before other nations. He has rejected the high sense of duty and obligation for the national body politic which pastors of the Japanese Christian Church must bear."[17]

Tamura rejected the Presbytery's disciplinary action and defended himself by saying that he had written out of a "spirit of love for the truth," pointing out that he had also praised certain aspects of Japanese culture in

14. Yuko, "The Changing Form of Dwellings."
15. Takeda, *The Yohohama Band's View of Women*, 10.
16. Enns, "Slander against Our People," 31–32.
17. Ibid., 33.

the book.[18] After refusing Tamura's request to present further witnesses, the Presbytery approved the investigative committee's decision by one vote.[19] Convinced of the rightness of his cause, Tamura appealed the decision to the Synod level that held a final meeting in July, 1894. After Uemura presented a statement in which he personally maligned Tamura for his unremitting, self-defensive attitude, the Synod affirmed the Presbytery's earlier decision and added an amendment mandating the ultimate punishment, Tamura's deposition from the ministry. The Synod's verdict read,

> The accused has behaved in a manner inappropriate for a minister. He has engaged in activities for which he has no authority, insulting the people and damaging the honor of the Japanese people before the nations. Instead of furthering the cause he is a serious obstacle to evangelism in Japan. Even though he received counsel on several occasions, he completely ignored this advice, refused to reconsider his behavior in any way and offered no apology. Instead, he rejected the counsel of others and defended himself, using whatever means were available. He has brought shame upon the position of minister in an ethical religion that requires the exercise of a high degree of personal responsibility. The first Meeting of the Tokyo Presbytery issued a very mild reprimand, requiring as punishment only that the author publish a correction in the appropriate magazines and newspapers. But he refused to accept even this. On the basis of the ample evidence which is available in the defendant's book itself, in the records of the Tokyo Presbytery, in the statements of both the plaintiff and the defendant before this session of the Synod, in the letter from the American, Mr. Phillips, and in an abundance of others facts, this meeting of the Synod amends the decision of the First Tokyo Presbytery. Mr. Tamura Naomi is not fit to serve as a minister. He is dismissed from his position as a minister.[20]

In his autobiography, Tamura described the Synod's action as "murder at the hands of the Yokohama Band."[21] Many of the missionaries present at the synod meeting were outraged and one yelled out, "Murder by a religious

---

18. Ibid, 32.
19. Ibid., 33.
20. Ibid., 35.
21. The Yokohama Band is a reference to the faction to which Uemura and Tamura's other accusers belonged. Tamura was from the Tsukiji Band, a competing Tokyo faction (Tamura, *Fifty Years of Faith*, 231).

court!" (*Shukyo hotei no satsujin!*). Later, the Council of Cooperating Missions issued the following carefully worded protest:

> The Council of Cooperating Missions has heard with profound regret the decision of the Diakwai of the Church of Christ in Japan deposing Rev. N. Tamura from the ministry. The reasons for the same are, that, while it must be admitted that there are statements and opinions presented in *The Japanese Bride*, which are open to criticism because of their lack of good taste and their unfairness, yet these statements and opinions have no relevance to any point of doctrine or government in the standards of the Church, nor, in the opinions of the members of this Council, can the writings of them be construed as a moral offense. Therefore, without expressing an opinion as to any alleged acts or statements of the Rev. N. Tamura, outside the formal charges preferred in the Diakwai, the sentence of deposition—the extreme penalty for the gravest offenses—is regarded as excessive, and as contrary to the spirit of love and justice.[22]

After the Synod's decision, Tamura and his congregation withdrew from the Japanese Presbyterians until rejoining them after Uemura's death in 1930. Tamura never retracted and continued pastoring the same church until his death in 1934. It is not an easy task to sort out the surface and depth dimensions of this case. Why were the Japanese church leaders, many of whom were themselves "progressives" in their views of women,[23] so quick to join the secular chorus of critics of Tamura and his book? Uemura himself had been a "strong advocate of family reform," and one of his daughters was the second woman ordained in the Presbyterian-Reformed tradition anywhere.[24] Was it Tamura's reputedly strong and individualistic personality that had incited the extreme reaction by his church? Indeed, Tamura's stubbornness flew in the face of the "community-first" relational loyalty that was assumed within the Confucian ethos of Meiji Japan. Or, given the lingering rivalry between the earliest Presbyterian Reformed factions (Tamura's Tsukiji Band vs. Uemura's Yokohama Band) and the fact that the Church of Christ in Japan (Presbyterian) had just been formed in 1890, was the book seized as a means for asserting the ecclesial dominance

---

22. From an unreferenced newspaper article in Tamura's personal file in the archives of Princeton Theological Seminary.

23. See Takeda, *The Yohohama Band's View of Women*, 20–24, for her analysis of the views of Uemura and Ibuka.

24. Enns, "Slander Against Our People," 29–30.

of Uemura's Yokohama Band? Furuya and Ohki conclude that, beyond these complex intrinsic issues, extrinsic political pressure was probably the greatest factor leading up to Tamura's deposition: "The greatest reason that this issue escalated to the level of an ecclesial trial was the self-preserving, opportunistic attitude of the church toward ultranationalism."[25]

Similarly claiming that the church made Tamura into a "fall guy" to assuage the wrath of the virulent nationalist critics of Christianity, Takeda says, "Rather than itself becoming the victim of the increasingly virulent emperor-centered nationalistic ideology, the recently founded Japanese church went too far in strategically trying to protect itself by daring to sacrifice one of its own, with the result that it is possible to conclude the young church was a 'tactician.'"[26]

For some time after this tragic incident, Tamura withdrew from public life and concentrated on his pastoral responsibilities at Sukiyabashi Church, his work with the students of the *Jieikan*, his reading, and gardening. Tamura's wife Eli later reported that Uchimura, the hapless victim of the *Lese Majesty Event*, was the only Japanese who visited Tamura during this exceedingly difficult time of exile.[27] They remained friends for life, and Uchimura himself said that Tamura was the only one who could really understand and comfort him because he, too, had been labeled as a traitor.[28] In spite of this period of "exile" following *The Japanese Bride* incident, Furuya and Ohki mistakenly conclude that Tamura, in contrast to his Yokohama Band rivals Uemura and Ibuka, "became a forgotten pastor."[29] On the contrary, not only did the Sukiyabashi Church grow under Tamura's pastoral leadership, three years after the incident he joined with other Christians in the public protest against the inhumane labor conditions at the Ashio Coal Mines. Tamura also participated in the mass evangelism campaign

---

25. Furuya and Ohki, *A Theology of Japan*, 126.
26. Takeda, *The Yohohama Band's View of Women*, 24.
27. Ibid., 11.
28. Furuya and Ohki, *A Theology of Japan*, 134.
29. Ibid., 120. This serious oversight by Ohki and Furuya is probably due to the fact that they are both systematic theologians. By contrast, in his 1935 *History of Modern Japanese Christians*, published one year after Tamura's death, Hiyane Antei not only includes Tamura in his list of the forty-one major leaders of the first generation of Japanese Protestants, but he makes more reference to Tamura than to other such noteworthies as Oshikawa, Nijima, and Yamamuro. The only nine leaders with more references than Tamura are Uemura, Uchimura, Ibuka, Ebina, Kanamori, Kozaki, Honda, Miyakawa, and Yokoi. This suggests that Tamura continued to be a dominant figure in the Japanese church long after *The Japanese Bride*. Antei, *History of Modern Japanese*.

launched by the Evangelical Federation in 1900 and,[30] more importantly, he became the leading Japanese interpreter and proponent of the religious education movement. Actually, it was his reading of the North American literature on the psychology of religion and the emergent religious education movement that rekindled Tamura's aspirations for the Christian transformation of Japanese society. For his choice of methods, Tamura turned from adult evangelism to the nurture of children, and from the direct, prophetic confrontation of his earlier work to a commitment to the long-term and indirect process of religious education. He has been called "the discoverer and liberator of Japan's children" and the "Comenius of Japanese Sunday School theory."[31]

FROM LIBERALISM TO ORTHODOXY

As far as I have been able to ascertain, my next case study is completely unknown in the English literature. Osaka Motokichiro[32] was born as the fifth son of the Hiratsuka family in Ishikawa Prefecture on June 25, 1880 and died June 10, 1945. He was later adopted by the Osaka family. While a student, he was strongly influenced by Nishida Kitaro (1875–1945), the famous Japanese philosopher and founder of the "Kyoto school." He entered the Department of Government at the Tokyo Imperial University in 1903. Though he was a zealous student of Zen while in Kanazawa, he lost interest after going to Tokyo after he started attending *Ichiban Cho* Church (later *Fujimi Cho*) and was baptized by Uemura Masahisa in 1904. For a short time, he was enrolled in Uemura's *Tokyo Shingakusha* (later Tokyo Union Theological Seminary), and after dropping out of Toyko Imperial University in 1908, left for the U.S. to pursue theological studies at Auburn Theological Seminary. In 1911 he went on to New College at Edinburgh and returned in 1912. In 1913, he became a minister of the Japan Christian Church (Presbyterian) and was ordained as the pastor of the Takeaway Church in Tokyo. He withdrew from the church when it split in 1917. He pioneered a church across from the factory at Osaki station, and in 1919, they held their commissioning ceremony as Osaki Church.

30. Akiyama, *Stories of Meiji-Era Personalities*, 21.
31. Tadashi, *Research on the Tsukiji Band*.
32. The information in this section draws heavily on the biographical section of Motokichiro, *The Collected Works*, 519–24; and Arimichi, gen. ed., *The Dictionary of the History of Japanese Christianity*.

Concerned about what he saw as the clannish church's indifference to the social evils of the day, Osaka advocated a "people's church" and in 1922, launched and presided over a progressively-minded study group called the Messiah Group. In 1917, he founded the magazine, *The Friend of Faith*, to promote the agenda of his Messiah Group. In 1925, at the invitation of an old high school friend, Osaka accepted a position as a contributor to the Religion Column in Yomiuri Newspaper and in 1929, he became the editor in chief for that column.

The Japanese Diet had initially proposed the passage of a Religious Bodies Law in 1927 and 1929, but after criticisms from both Buddhists and Christians, the bill had been temporarily shelved. While the government claimed that the law was intended not to restrict but to protect religion, subsequent events reveal that it was intended as a way to centrally regulate all religious bodies while granting favored status for Shinto shrines associated with the imperial household. Beginning in 1929, Osaka repeatedly attempted to critically comment in his Yomiuri column on the law in the hopes of obstructing its passage. Since the bill had already been shelved twice, the government and the shrines redoubled their efforts and in December, 1929, the Diet established an ad-hoc "Shrine System Investigative Committee" appointing Yamagawa Kenjiro as chair and Imaizumi Josie as a member. This was the period of time when the so-called Shrine Issue[33] was popping up all over the country, and Osaka was persistent in using his column in the Yomiuri to voice his critical comments.

While continuing to use the newspaper column in the fight for the blockage of the Religious Bodies Law and to comment on the Shrine Issue, Osaka made a convincing case that Buddhists and Christians were in complete agreement on this line of attack. Like many other Japanese Christians of the time, Osaka believed that inter-religious dialogue was essential to the formation of a modern, democratic Japan. At the same time, the real editorial intention of the conservative newspaper was to cultivate a feeling of suspicion and animosity toward the politically idealistic and naive Rev. Osaka. In a February 1934 column, Osaka took the Shrine Observance Committee headed by Imaizumi to task, charging that Imaizumi's group was a quasi-religion that did not actually represent either the shrines or any of the thirteen Shinto sects and was an enigmatic religious group unjustly protected by civic law. This raised the ire of Imaizumi.

33. The "Shrine Issue" refers to the government's requirement that all Japanese school children participate in religious observances at shrines associated with the emperor.

In March, Imaizumi called on Osaka, who was at work in the newspaper's office, and enticed him into his car. He was taken to the Daijingu in Idabashi, an imperial shrine that is famous for weddings. Once there, four or five of Imaizumi's underlings surrounded Osaka, sat him in the direction of the shrine and demanded he apologize for and recant what he had written in his newspaper columns. When Osaka refused, the men attacked him, grabbed his neck, and forced him to bow toward the shrine. Then they began to pummel Osaka's ribs. After a while, saying they were all going to make up now, they got Osaka back into the car and took him next to the Meiji Shrine at Gaien, and adding insult to injury, they hit him on the head and broke his ribs. Osaka barely survived what he later said were karate chops aimed and his weak spots which were clearly intended to kill him. As a result of this attack, Osaka, who had never been sick before, was long confined to his sickbed, and his disease evolved from pleurisy caused by external trauma into degeneration of the rib bones.

His physical ailments were extremely rare, virulent, and harsh. On the 9th floor of the Police Hospital, Osaka received one operation after another and fell in and out of critical condition. He was visited in the hospital by his former teacher Nishida and some friends. During a recovery process that he called "receiving one life for nine deaths," he gradually made a turn for the better. Requiring constant medical care for a year and a half, the healing process was extremely difficult. During that period, his friend Shoriki Matsutaro, a well-known politician and businessman, helped cover his hospital expenses.

Osaka received the following two notes from Nishida during his hospitalization:

> "According to your postcard, it seems you truly barely managed to escape from danger with your life. At one point I was truly worried. I think you will need to really take care of yourself much more than before the need for all of those operations." . . . "I read your letter. I was really worried about you at one point and am so happy to hear of your wonderful recovery. I think it is impossible for you to come here now, but I will be waiting for your visit next spring."

According to what Osaka said later to many friends, he thought he was going to be murdered when they forced him to bow his head at that shrine. Commenting on Osaka's ordeal, Ishiguro writes, "The essence of this event was exactly the same kind of victimization or persecution of faith which Paul experienced when he attacked Artemis and incited the wrath of Demetrius, the silver smith (cf. Acts 19:23–24)."

What did Osaka experience during this terribly long time of suffering? We can hear Osaka's own account from the various greetings he wrote to people while hospitalized.

> Last year in March I met with an unexpected disaster. Since then I again and again fell into pleurisy that finally led to degeneration of my rib and head bones. Suffering muscular degeneration, I had to have six operations, during which time I fell into erysipelas ("a local febrile disease accompanied by diffused inflammation of the skin, producing a deep red color, often called St. Anthony's fire or 'the rose.'" *OED*). In spite of all this, I have recovered by the wonder of God's grace. (October, 1935)

He wrote in more detail to his church in their bulletin after his sickness:

> My sickness began with two bouts of pleurisy and led to degeneration of the rib and head bones. Before and after I the experience of muscle inflammation and motion sickness, I had a total of nine operations. During that time, I fell into the serious condition of erysipelas. In particular, during the first operation for rib bone degeneration, they had planned to remove my first rib only, but after cutting and opening me, they discovered that the degeneration had spread to the fourth rib, and after administering local anesthetic again and again, they continued the operation. There are no words to describe the pain I experienced. Groaning upon the operating table drenched in sweat and blood, I was assaulted by the idea, "Why must we suffer?" At the same time I called to mind all of my past sins and as a response, I worshipped before the Divine presence at God's judgment seat. God was now using the hands of the doctors to strike me. This severe pain was being applied completely and everywhere without stopping, and I earnestly looked into the face of that solemn and severe Divine presence and fixed my gaze on Him. My heart was overwhelmed with a sense of repentance. (August 20, 1937)

As we can see from Osaka's own words, the ordeal turned out to be not only an experience of physical illness, but also a deep religious experience. During his sickness, while he was pondering God's judgment, he also began to recognize the sacredness of the human spirit and bitterly grieved over his own sinfulness. Further, he prayed earnestly for the chance to once again serve people if God healed him of his illness. He saw all this as a profound, mystical experience, and Osaka rose up from his sick bed a different person. From this point on, Osaka started drawing a sharp line with his former way of life.

The first communication from Osaka after his sickness reads: "I have for the first time known the strict impartiality of Heaven. I am in fearful awe. I am fighting sin with fear." (February 13, 1935) The core issue upon which he had acutely reflected before and after the three years he spent lying in bed was that his own faith up till that point had been excessively conceptual and philosophical. Before his transformation, he had acted wisely with a Christianity as a cultural or philosophical phenomena without ever delving into the meaning of Christ's salvation. He had seen Christianity as a kind of a this-worldly philosophical or social movement. He concluded that the reason he had not wondered about what real salvation was about was because he had never pondered the question of ecclesiology. He realized that he had neither learned this from his elders nor been enlightened on his own and, as a result, he believed that he had lived his life up to the time of his trial to the detriment of himself and others. However, even though he realized that his transformation was belated, he believed it was not too late to begin anew from the present. He decided to devote the remainder of his life to correcting the mistakes of his past and endeavoring to clearly disclose the truth of Christianity.

After being released from the hospital, Osaka had to spend the first year at home convalescing. Gradually, his health returned and from the fall of 1936, he began attending Osaki Church in Musashino Oyama until he was finally able to stand in the pulpit to preach. At the same time, he began to devote himself to a life immersed in reading, prayer, and religious practice. In those days, Osaka used to tell the members of his church, "From here on out I will pour out all of my strength into the church. Always waiting expectantly and with awe for the coming Lord, looking to the Lord on high, searching ourselves deeply, let us remember the Lord's Body in our midst. Further, let us consider ourselves as a monastic community."

As is evident in these words, after being released from the hospital, Osaka made a firm decision to begin to seek an embodied, holistic piety.

One of the members of his church later wrote,

> At first he started reading Kierkegaard after his release from the hospital but found that it left something to be desired, so he decided to turn to Augustine. He borrowed the complete works of Augustine from his close friend and read them again and again. The

intensity of spirit with which he read was amazing. He said that he discovered that his own quest for and experience of salvation during his sickness was mirrored in Augustine's own experience of faith and perfectly described theologically. He was overwhelmed by Augustine's theology. For example, while he was reading *On the Trinity*, since every single word seemed to be in sympathetic correspondence with his own experience during his sickness, and he said that he sometimes couldn't keep his hand from shaking as he turned the next page. When Osaka realized there were many other early theologians with whom Augustine was in sympathy, he knew that reading Augustine alone was insufficient. He felt the need to go back directly to the source of the tradition. From this point he devoted himself to the intensive study of the Ante Nicean and Post Nicean Fathers that were collected in an English edition of more than ten volumes. His desire for study in those days was truly stupendous. Presumably, the acquisition and purchase of that series cost him a great deal or perhaps he had some financial assistance from someone. He searched for them in some used book stores in Tokyo, and avidly read whatever he could get his hands on.

In this way he read the church fathers, and after being immersed in them for a number of years, he gained a certain conviction concerning what all the church's early theologians had experienced. Namely, the witness to what Osaka called the "catholic experience" of being linked as an embodied branch to the root and trunk of the Triune God through the mediation of the Incarnate Christ. Precisely because the early theologians of the church had been able to experience the transformation of salvation in Christ, they were able to hold fast to the faith to the point of the shedding of martyr's blood and to effectively pass on the faith. For Osaka, the great procession of Ignatius, Polycarp, Ireneaus, Origen, Tertullian, Cyprian, Athanasius, the three Cappadocian fathers, and Augustine were like a shining galaxy in the dark world of pre-WWII Japan. Osaka drew the conclusion that the core tradition of the Christian Church had been formed by the fourth century during that vigorous phase of development. As a result, he saw that the only place to which we must also return is to the church before split of both the Eastern and Western churches. He emphasized that this is the "catholic church" confessed in both the Apostles' Creed and the Nicene Creed. It seemed like a long road, but this time after going through this painful personal ideal, he finally arrived at what he had been searching for since his youth, and his heart danced with deep emotion and joy that he had at last struck the vein of truth.

Osaka's ascetic praxis was not limited to reading and writing. As a way to encourage others in the life of faith, he decided that he must practically exemplify a life of devoted service. From August in 1937, he built a small room adjoining the church sanctuary with a bed and there he slept, waking every morning at four a.m., and spent the entire day concentrated on prayer and study. This was his daily round while he was intensively reading the church fathers. From the beginning of this ascetic lifestyle, there were those who wondered how long he could keep it up, but it lasted till March 1944 when the war was drawing to a close and there was great turmoil. During that long period, Osaka was in the church twenty-four hours a day, and of course he poured his greatest effort into Sunday worship, but also never missed the prayer discipline of three daily prayer meetings, held together with a few laypeople early in the morning, at three in the afternoon and again at seven in the evening. He also lectured on the Lord's Prayer and the Nicene, Apostles', and Athanasian Creed.

A pamphlet he published in November 1938 titled "An Ascetic Memoir of the Season of Christ's Advent," expresses his indefatigable devotion to the life of piety. He sent a copy of that pamphlet to his beloved teacher Nishida Kitaro who wrote back, "My heart was set ablaze on one reading of the pamphlet which you sent."

Having briefly introduced the stories of Tamura and Osaka, I want to now point out some of the complex and creative tensions and dangers that may surface when dreams inspired by crossing over postal-codes confront conflicting aspirations and realities. In order to grasp these complex dynamics, I will consider the cases of Tamura and Osaka while referring to Roland Robertson's model of the "global field."[34] This brilliant model provides a *comparative interactive* perspective that is very helpful in a diachronic analysis of the relativizing tensions that accompanied the missionary transmission of the Christian message in Japan and can be clearly seen in the two cases we have presented.

In terms of social, political, and cultural capital, the fledging Japanese churches of Tamura and Osaka's time were a dramatic contrast to the North American churches which had both the means and motivation to send and support missionaries to far away places like Japan. Tamura and Osaka's cases show that the nascent minority Japanese Protestant churches embodied a complex confluence of personal, national, international, and universal

---

34. See Robertson, *Globalization*, 27.

factors (see Robertson's model). The stories of Tamura and Osaka, and many others, reflect these daunting relativizing or "exilic" tensions.

The Japanese Bride became such a controversy because Tamura drew on U.S. marriage practices and Christian ethical ideals to boldly criticize and demythologize local Japanese practices. In his public advocacy for a greater degree of religious freedom in pre-war Japan, Osaka similarly drew on the achievements and ideals of the social gospel movement in North America, hoping to relativize his nation's march toward nationalism. It is important to call to mind the overwhelming political, economic, and cultural influence that the Western powers wielded during the late nineteenth and early twentieth centuries. Also, it was precisely the global expansion of Western power that helped underwrite and transmit the project of modernity. Further, while it is partly an anachronism to call the missionaries colonialists or imperialists, the modern missionary movement would have been unthinkable without the political, economic, and cultural hegemony of the Western powers. Needless to say, the missionaries were bearers and transmitters of the distinctive societal traditions of their homelands as well as of their particular understanding of the gospel of Jesus Christ. This meant that the highly literate and patriotic early generations of Japanese church leaders like Tamura and Osaka had to struggle to sort out their own understanding of the gospel within the turbulent, cross-postal code confluence of the following four major factors:

1. Their relation to the missionaries and the Western churches and societies who sent them (relativization of societal reference);

2. Their approach to contemporary intellectual developments in the West (relativization of societal reference);

3. Their desire to see their churches become strong and independent (individual-society problematic);

4. Their hopes for their beloved Japan to become a strong modern nation-state (individual-society problematic).

There are surely many other untold narratives from the non-Western churches that will greatly enrich our current conversation on postcodes.

WORKS CITED

Akiyama, S. *Stories of Meija-Era Personalities: A Genealogy of Christianity.* Tokyo: Shiny, 1982. [in Japanese]

Ante, H. *History of Modern Japanese Christians.* Tokyo: Kirisutokyo Shisogyosho, 1935. [in Japanese]

Ennis, R. "Slander against Our People: Tamura Naomi and the Japanese Bride Incident." *Japanese Religions* 18 (1993) 15–46.

Motokichiro, O. *The Collected Works.* Tokyo: Shiny, 1971. [in Japanese]

Ebisawa Arimichi, general editor. *The Dictionary of the History of Japanese Christianity.* Tokyo: Kyobunkan, 1988.

Kiyoko, T. *The Yohohama Band's View of Women: Reflections on the Japanese Bride Incident.* Tokyo: Meiji Gakuin University Institute for Christian Studies, 1997. [in Japanese]

Naomi, T. *Fifty Years of Faith.* Tokyo: Keiseisha, 1924. [in Japanese]

———. *The Japanese Bride,* New York: Harper & Brothers, 1893.

Robertson, R. *Globalization: Social Theory and Global Culture.* Theory, Culture & Society. London: Sage, 1992.

Sanneh, L. *Translating the Message: The Missionary Impact on Culture.* American Society of Missiology Series 13. Maryknoll, NY: Orbis, 1989.

Tadashi, M., editor. *Research on the Tsukiji Band.* Tokyo: UCCJ Sugamo Church, 1986. [in Japanese]

Yuko, N. "The Changing Form of Dwellings and the Establishment of the Katei (Home) in Modern Japan." *U.S.-Japan Women's Journal* 8 (1995). Online: http://www.petroway.com/usjwj/toce.htm.

www.ingramcontent.com/pod-product-compliance
Lightning Source LLC
Chambersburg PA
CBHW051940160426
43198CB00013B/2235